YEHUWAY'S LAWS, 2016

WALTER JOSEPH SCHENCK, JR.

Yehuway's Laws, 2016
Copyright © 2016
Walter Joseph Schenck, Jr.

This is a work of fiction. Names, characters, places, and incidents either are the product of the author's imagination or are used fictitiously, and any resemblance to actual persons, living or dead, events, or locales is entirely coincidental.

Excepts of text formerly published in
Priests & Warriors by Walter Joseph Schenck, Jr.

ISBN-13: 978-1532711992
ISBN-10: 1532711999

CreateSpace Independent Publishing Platform, North Charleston, SC

To Mankind who have lost their way

Contents

CHAPTER

1

Land of Yisra'el

HERE IS WHAT I, the Paraclete, have been instructed to write by Yehuway.

"'I, Yehuway, will preserve the Land of Yisra'el. I will do this for the sake of Abraham. I will do this for the sake of the righteous ones who now wear the clothes of Abraham, even if they are not born directly from the loins of Abraham. I will do this for the sake of those people who have journeyed through trial and anguish to come to me through My son Yehohshua. It is I, Yehuway, who has appointed Yehohshua to be the chief Mashi'ach. Yehohshua is My law enforcer.

"'I, Yehuway, will command for you, the children of righteousness to receive an eternal blessing – yes, for you and for your storehouses. Yes, a blessing that will touch everything that you set your hand to perform. I will bless you in the land which I, Yehuway, your true and only God, have set aside for you.'

"Listen to me, spiritual inheritors of Yehuway's blessing: Yehuway will establish for Himself a holy people that will obey Him with righteous actions in all things. For this, He has sworn to them, 'If you keep My commandments, yes, every law that I, Yehuway, your true and only God, have written, and if you continuously walk in My ways, you will be preserved into a prosperous life.'

"The great and expectant result is this, all people of the earth; yes, without exception, who call upon the name of Yehuway—whether from the loins of Abraham or not—will cause their enemies to be afraid of them. Even the demons will tremble and run away from you.

"Yehuway will fulfill you in vast prosperity. All the materialism that you desire will come about. You will have health in the fruit of your body. You will not suffer from a weak heart or from the rapid deterioration of your body or from malignant diseases, or from any other sort of ailments. Even the health of your livestock will be preserved. People and livestock will flourish in a rich and vibrant earth. All vegetables and all fruit trees will grow in the land that Yehuway has sworn to your fathers to give to you.

"Yehuway will open to you His good treasure. The heavens will release the rains and the mists to your land during the fall and during the summer. Even the winters will become mild, without affliction. Yehuway will bless all the works of your hand. Yisra'el will lend monies, talents, and intellect to many nations. The Children of Yisra'el, both spiritual and physical, will never have to borrow money nor depend upon the pity of others. Israel will become the generous nation upon whom all the other nations will depend.

"Yehuway will make you the head, not the tail, and you will be above the peoples of the earth. No, you will not be beneath them. This will happen if you listen to the commandments of Yehuway your true and only God.

"Listen to His voice: 'I command you on this day: Observe and obey My laws. Do not stray away from My laws or from any of My words that I command to you this day. Align the right hand so the left hand may obey My commandments. Do not turn your thoughts to anything other than what I am presenting to you, people of the earth. Do not go after other gods to serve you. They are false and pretentious. Wicked demons inhabit the icons and marble statues and paintings that pretend to portray godly representation. Satan lies deviously through all such images. There are no exceptions. All icons are bitter and foul. Do not believe that I am the god of all religions and churches. I am not! I cannot tolerate men of any religious belief killing men from that same affiliation. The Children of Ismael kill others to preserve their false beliefs. I grow tired and incensed at you. Black men commit heinous crimes against other black men. I grow tired and incensed at you. White prejudice prevails over everything intolerable to their set motions. I also grow tired and incensed at you.

"'All of you are flatterers of yourselves. You feed your own false pretenses. Hear me, O Yisra'el: I am not the same god that every church spokesperson wants you to believe I am. I do not love every religion or variant philosophical thoughts. In fact – I despise them. They are abhorrent to Me. I have vowed to Myself and to my righteous children to destroy their buildings, their books, the men within, the wives and sons and daughters, and, yes, even their newborns, because I do not originate from the mind and substance of man! A cosmic explosion did not create me and the universe does not ignite in repetitious rebirth and death. Creation came about only once—and I alone saw to it. Everything exists solely because I have performed it to be. Listen to me: it is I, Yehuway the singular God, who has created humankind. For eons, I journeyed alone in deepest emptiness where nothing that is now was. I did not even have a Son. I took a part out from My own entity, and with that powerful withdrawal of energy, I created My first life – yes, My only begotten son who is known as Jesus Christ. Jesus Christ is revealed by Me to you as Mikha'el the Archangel. It is I who empowered My Son to stand beside Me. I shared My energy of energies with him. I love him so much I directed his mouth to speak a singular word: LIFE. Thereafter, began the formulation of everything that came to be. Yes, before that moment, not even the stars shone. The waters that now nourish you did not flow from the mountaintops. Nothing—anywhere—is remotely equal to Me. Thus, I am not a god who seeks the affections of vain pretenders and false leaders who carve insane icons from cold marble: a stone that I can with the smallest thought, render into dust. I am the only True God. I alone sustain life. Yes, it is true; your life came directly from My energy. All that you are was nothing until I made it so.

"'Your human parents, I, Yehuway, created from the elements of the earth. My Son, whom I dearly love, whose true identity is Mikha'el the Archangel, I authorized to assist Me in their formation. That is why Mikha'el the Archangel is authorized as my speaker to mankind, as symbolized by Aharon being the spokesperson for Moshe.

"'Listen to me, people of the earth, whether you are born from the loins of Abraham or born from another tribe, it will happen that if you do not obey My voice, I, Yehuway your true and only God, will bring terrible punishments on you. All the curses that I have ever pronounced over the centuries against you, will now come against you as an amplification of regret. War and pestilence will overtake you.

"'Observe My commandments. Obey My statutes that I have written for you in My books. Do not permit the demons to take you away from My presence and lead you into a cursed path. Do not be misled to live in

11

an unholy city filed with wickedness. Why make life miserable where you end up farming a land filled with rotting fruits and vegetables? Yes, their filth fills the air with a hideous stench. I am a God of Life. Not a God of Sorrow.

"'Disobey Me and this will be the consequence: Your places of business will fail. Your merchandise will sit unsold and the worm will consume the foods that you have purchased for resale. All of your business ventures will become unproductive. Those of you who nevertheless achieved vast wealth did not do so through My blessings, but, rather, through satanic affiliation. What business, what government, what society carries My blessings? None. None, that is, except the eternal Nation of Yisra'el.

"'Your human bodies age unpleasantly because you have failed to obey Me. You suffer ill health because you failed to hear My words in your hearts. The vegetables, the fruit, and the shade of the trees wither and die because you think your talents are greater than My blessings. Fewer children will be born from the womb of your wife. The flocks of your sheep will go hungry as they thin.

"'You will be hated whenever you walk outside your home. Yes, you will be hated, even if you step outside for a brief moment. The same will happen even as you seek the confines of the walls of your house. The hatred of all the world's population will follow you inside.'

Listen again to Yehuway's words. These words are a dire warning for the Children of the earth if they fail to love, honor, and respect Yehuway. These warnings are eternal, given to all humans of all nations.

"Yehuway will send upon you a curse, a vexation – a rebuke in everything that you set your hand to do, even until you are destroyed. Yes, to the actual point where you will quickly perish. This will occur if you are wicked in what you perform and because your doings have forsaken Yehuway.

"Yehuway will make the pestilence cleave to you, until He has consumed you completely off the land that was originally set aside for you to possess.

"Yehuway will smite you with consumption, with a fever, with an inflammation, with an extreme burning, with the sword, with blasting, with mildew. Yes, the nations of the unholy will perish.

"The very heavens, the white clouds that moisten your heads, will seem as white-hot brass. The waterless region and unrelenting heat will become a terrible burden. The earth that you walk upon will seem a white-hot iron.

"Yehuway will transform the sweet rains that fall into bitter acid. The morning mist that once hovered over your land will vanish to sheer waves of dry heat. The fertile topsoil of your lands will become powdered dust. The heavens will cease to gather the rain clouds that had adorned your lands with vast vegetation. You will reside in a land possessed with rocks and clay until you are destroyed.

"Yehuway will take away the energies of your life. Your murdered and deranged corpses will litter the breath and depths of the land. Yes, each of your enemies will slaughter you and your children and wives and newborns. Your armies will travel in a single, senseless direction against those who charge against you. The disobedient armies will fall in disarray. I will conquer the apostate nations will vanquish them in seven directions. What greater amusement for me than to see it become so? It will occur; the nations will be removed from the earth. All former nations will become a singular country, the Kingdom of Yehuway. My angels will rise as a mighty army to afflict you if you are not careful about preserving within yourselves My instructions. The nations that oppose my laws shall be afflicted. Remember, I wanted to preserve the Children of Yisra'el against all enemies. Do not turn away from Me, so I in turn, may never turn away from Yaakov, your forefather who I had cherished. He, because of my love for his father Isaac and forefather Abraham, anointed him to father the twelve tribes that would inhabit the Land of Yis'rael."

℠℠℠℠℠℠

The Paraclete continues: "The uncountable carcasses that fill the donkey driven carts of once living and thriving flesh will become meat for all the fowls of the air. Yes, even the hyenas, the dogs, and the pigs will eat the flesh of my enemies. No one will attempt to push them away.

"Yehuway will smite you with the damaging onslaught from heaven. Your bodies will become afflicted with hemorrhoids, with scabs, and with an unrelenting itch between your legs. A terrible rash will afflict your arms and face. No medicine will heal you.

"Yehuway will smite you with insanity and incurable afflictions. The people will lose the sight of their eyes and become toothless. Yes, the hearts of the wicked disobeyers of the Law will become astonished by the sheer strength of Yehuway's curse.

"The wicked person will grope at noonday, as the blind grope in darkness. The insincere person will not prosper in anything he strives to perfect. His only accomplishment will be the soil of oppression that overtakes his life. No man can save the manipulator and averter of truth. Those who live in omission of the one true God will themselves become omitted from eternal life.

"Listen to these truths. A husband will marry a wife, yet another man will go to bed with her and have pleasurable intercourse with her. You will build a house, however, you will not live in that house. You will plant a vineyard, yet you will not gather even a single grape.

"Your children will be slain before your eyes. Yes, it will occur that you will become grateful to your enemy if that enemy permits you to eat a single slice of meat from the ox's maggot infected degenerate and filthy carcass. Your home will be violently stolen from you, yes, even in front of your face. Though you know the thieves, your home will not be restored to you. Your possessions shall be given to your enemies, and you will not find a single hero to help you restore them back to you.

"Your sons and your daughters will be murdered by terrorist with an insatiable insanity to hurt anyone they can, regardless of belief, wealth, gender, age. Yes, Yehuway will permit other nations to accomplish your destruction and dispersal. Your eyes will look, but they will fail to understand what is occurring around you. no matter how much you study the events. Your relatives and children will suffer. The will become separated from you in the middle of chaotic events. Search for them all day. It will not avail you. Your hand is weak, without strength."

Yehuway's Action Against an Opposer

The Paraclete, directly inspired through the Holy Spirit, modernizes and interpolates: "The fruit of the opposers to Yisra'el, the Iranians, the Syrians, the Egyptians, the Saudis, along with all their labors, will be surrendered to the Russians who will be permitted to disperse you. Russia will turn against Syria and Iran because this promise I make: the Iranians and the Palestians will never prevail against you.

"Again, what your opposers have planted, they will not eat. The Kurdistan will rise, though they had fallen through the lies of the sons of the British. The Kurdistan armies will oppress and crush Tukey and Syria and Iraq. Their children are the descendants of Ephraim. France, Belgium, Germany will seek a solution to the European crises, but they will not discover a solution, for it is already too late. However, my believers, my faithful, my adherents will be gathered as a hen gathers her offspring and they will take possession of a new earth restored with vineyards and bountiful harvests. The Garden of Eden which I had presented to the original parents to occupy as an eternal gift of righteousness from the one and only true God who loves His children of obedience will grow from one sector of the earth to the remotest sector of the earth."

Yehuway again speaks through the mouth of Mikha'el the Archangel.

"The swiftness of these events will enrage the children of the parents who will ask how their own parents—and their own grandparents—could have turned away so greatly from the true God to encounter such a terrible punishment to witness the final day of retribution. For the children who of the parents who had trusted in me, I, Yehuway, will perform their salvation from the day of wrath so they may will not suffer the punishments that I will meld out to the unbelievers.

"The faithful parents who had experienced an insanity of lawlessness, though they may have perished, will be restored to life in the times of the resurrection. They will ask forgiveness from Me and from the person they transgressed against. The seeker of forgiveness will receive forgiveness. No one will withhold his or her embraces of love. Happy smiles and fresh eyes will renew hopes and wonder and love – everyone will become an innocent person.

"The detestable thing that I, Yehuway, will perform against the wicked will be so vast; the people of the earth will become consumed by a rage of unfathomable consequences. They will wake in a maddened state at the things they will witness in front of their eyes. These things they will remember, and they will speak of it to the children born after the final assault of My angels against the nations of the earth.

"I, Yehuway will smite the opposers in the knees, in the legs, in the toes, in the arms, in the hands, and in the fingers. They will suffer a terrible soreness that cannot be healed. Yes, even from the soles of their feet to the top of their heads. I, Yehuway will bring them and the leaders that had subjected you to their vices and unreasonable dictates down to the shades of Sheol, an eternal death from which none can escape. My believers, my faithful I will escort to a nation that neither you nor your fathers have known. I, Yehuway, speak of the future Kingdom of Yehuway. Therein, my precious children will forget the false gods carved from worthless wood and stone. They are blind, lacking in spirituality.

"How can I, Yehuway, permit a people that has betrayed Me to know of Me once they have left Me? I will see to it that they forget how to pronounce and spell My own True name. The betrayers will become astonished at what has befallen them. Those who survive the ordeal may be likened to a proverb, a byword, among all the nations where I will purpose them to be dispersed to.

"Listen, opposers, you will carry a bagful of healthy seeds out into the field, but only a few seeds will grow. Their performance will come to naught because the locust will consume the vast majority of seeds.

"You will plant vineyards, cultivate, and care for them, but you will neither drink the wine nor gather the grapes, for the worms will eat them.

"You will plant olive trees throughout your coasts, but you will not anoint yourself with the oil. The olive tree will lose its fruit.

"Sons and daughters will be born to you, but you will not enjoy their presence or activities because the false rulers of the world will enslave you with deceptive promises of economic gains, housing, food, medical help, a strong infrastructure, and technological advances that do nothing more than serve the leaders of the nations who are against me.

"The stranger who lives among you will establish himself as your ruler. The migrant occupier will rise in power, as your own power is lost to become a faint memory of former grandeur.

"Yes, it will be the occupier who will lend money, talent, and intellect to you. You will not be the one who lends him the money. He will become the head, while you become the tail.

"Moreover, all these curses will come upon you. The outsiders who were never meant to reside in the lands I have entrusted to you will then pursue you until they overtake you! Yes, even until you are destroyed. All this will happen if you do not listen to the voice of Yehuway, our true and only God. All this will happen if you fail to keep His commandments and His statutes, which He has commanded you to obey. These unrelenting curses will come upon you and become a thing of extreme wonder upon your seed forever if you fail to serve Yehuway, your God, with a joyful heart and with a resolute commitment of mind and body.

ॐ☙ॐ☙ॐ☙ॐ☙ॐ☙

"Perform with a glad heart obedience to Yehuway so you may obtain and preserve the abundance of all things.

"Do these things and you will never have to serve your enemies, if you are pure in your heart and perform all things in accordance with Yehuway's Laws. Whom then can Yehuway send against you? You will never suffer hunger nor experience thirst. Your body will never be naked. Your house will never be empty of material goods. Do not perform the things that Yehuway has commanded you, and He will place a yoke of iron over your neck until He has destroyed you.

"Ignore the laws and Yehuway will energize His son to lead a vast army of angels to war against you. This army will stem from the foundations of heaven. The destroying warriors will come against you with a great horde from heaven, yes, even from the end of the cosmos, as swift as the eagle can fly. This army will speak in a tongue that you will not understand so they cannot hear your pleads for mercy, for they shall have none. This army will be empowered by Yehuway to manifest throughout the world a fierce countenance.

Prior to this act of righteousness to cleanse the earth from evil, Yehuway will step aside so the demons may, at their own pleasure, influence the leaders and the populace against all good virtues and proper principles and concerns for righteousness. The demons will address its own laws without regard to the respect of the common citizen. One percent will rule ninety-nine percent. It will not show concern toward you or your loved ones no matter if you are an old person or a young person. No favors will be granted.

"The conqueror will eat the meat from your cattle as well as the fruits of your land until you are destroyed. When he vacates the land, the soldier and the occupier will not leave you barley, wine, or oil. It will be a desolate land that he will vacate. You will no longer give birth to children, and the flocks of your sheep will lessen until the conqueror has destroyed you.

"This enemy will besiege you in all your gates until your great walls come crashing down. The walls and fortifications that you have trusted in will betray you. Every city, throughout the land, will have a terrible war raging against it until all the gates of all your cities that

Yehuway, our true and only God has given you, will have fallen to the enemy.

"Listen more to this terrible anguish, this nightmare that can become an absolute reality: Visualize yourselves amputating and consuming your own legs and arms. Yes, see in the depths of your minds the harsh reality of you eating the flesh of your sons and daughters, which Yehuway, our true and only God has given to you, during the time of the horrific siege. In an unimaginable truth, your enemies will distress you beyond belief. The folly will be so terrible it will render the gentle person who lives among you, no matter how delicate, to turn his eye to perform evil acts upon his own brother. Yes, the gentle man will do terrible things against his pledged wife, the very woman whom he adores and loves with all his heart. This once tender and merciful man will hate the remainder of his children. He will abandon them.

"The gentle man and kind woman will not share their food with any of them. Both will discard the flesh of their children. Yes, the father and the mother will murder their sons and daughters. Both of them will eat their children's legs and arms because they have nothing left inside them but rage toward everything and everyone. The enemy's siege, in all its unimaginable terribleness, will distress you in all your gates.

"Similarly, the tender and merciful woman who resides among you, who would never have ventured beyond the refuge of her sanctity or set the sole of her foot upon the ground because of her delicate tenderness, yes, even her eye will become evil toward the husband who had been pledged to her. She will hate her son as well as her daughter. She will hate her newly born child that just came come out from between her legs. She will be filled with rage at everything her children perform to whom she has given birth. Like the man, she, herself, will slay her sons and daughters. She will knife their flesh from their legs and arms, and she will eat their flesh because of the hunger that afflicts her. The secret things that had been performed in the safety of the bedrooms will be exposed to the eyes of the enemy who will distress you in your gates.

"If you fail to observe each word of the law that has been written in this book, the consequences will be direr than you can possibly image. I urge you to respect and honor the glorious name of our Divine Yehuway. Not to do so creates a portentous fear without reckoning.

"When you think the worst of the worst has passed, more strife will come yet against you. Yehuway will increase your plagues. You and your seed will suffer great plagues of long continuance. Yes, horrible sicknesses of long continuance will settle throughout the land.

"More yet: He will bring upon you by a factor of ten thousand times ten thousand all the diseases of Egypt that surely had once before made all of you tremble throughout those arduous times. Do not pretend that you are unafraid. All these evils will cleave to you–every sickness, yes, even every plague that is not written in the Book of Law, Yehuway will bring upon you until you are destroyed."

ಬಌಣಬಌಣಬಌಣಬಌಣ

The Paraclete, directly inspired through the Holy Spirit, now interpolates: "When the great Japhethite nation that rose from the midst of agonized vengeance completes its task, then Yehuway Himself will condemn it in return for the treachery it perpetrated throughout the world. Yehuway will unleash His heavenly, unconquerable military might against it. Among the seven billion humans, only a few will survive the greatest calamities in history. Men, women, children, and newborns will perish. The horrific terrors will resonate throughout the universe only to settle to a deafened God. The final generation of human beings who had numbered in the land as the stars of heaven, will barely remain. All this will occur because you did not obey the voice of Yehuway, your God.

"This will happen: Just as Yehuway had once delighted to rejoice over you and who had personally performed unselfishly good deeds for you—even to multiply you—so Yehuway will rejoice in His destruction over you. Yehuway will bring you to a state of utter nothingness. You will be plucked from the land that has been set aside for Abraham's heirs to inherit. What was once yours to possess – for a time in history, you will not possess. However, a portion of the land will be returned to you in the final event of the worldly governments' existence."

"Disobey Yehuway and He will scatter you among the people of the earth, yes even from one end of the earth to the other. In those foreign lands, you will be entreated to serve other gods, which neither you nor your fathers have known, even gods of wood and stone – and you will acquiesce to them.

"You will be scattered to reside among the foreign nations where you will never find comfort. Neither will the sole of your feet take a brief repose. Yehuway will cause you to suffer a trembling heart as well as a failure of your eyes. Your mind will suffer terrible sorrow. A never ending depression. A paranoia of an endless loss of your identity. An irreconcilable distress will afflict you and your life will hang in doubt before you. You will tremble in fear throughout the day and night. There will not be a single second of peace for you or a single assurance of your life lingering for a moment more.

"In the morning you will say, 'Will God permit me to see the evening sunset?'

"In the evening, you will say, 'Will God permit me to see the sunrise? I am afraid. My heart has no rest from fear. My eyes are afraid of everything they see.'

"Yehuway will return you to oppressive lands similar to Egypt where you will suffer miserable torment and abusive practices against you. This time your children will be enslaved inside slave ships because of the course of action that you have practiced against Yehuway's good laws that I, the Paraclete, have revealed to you."

ಬುಲ್ಬುಲ್ಬುಡುಬುಲ್ಬುಲ್

Yehuway now speaks through the mouth of Mikha'el the Archangel.

"Disobey me and you will not be permitted to enter into paradise which I had set aside for you. In the final moments of your desired entry, you will be gathered together by your enemies to be murdered. What human being can rescue you?"

CHAPTER

2

THESE ARE THE WORDS revolving around the second covenant.

Listen Only to Yehuway

Yehuway told the Paraclete to study Moshe *Rabbenu's* writing to present this second treaty about moral performance and allegiance to the Children of Yisra'el while they resided in the land of Moab. The first covenant, Yehuway had presented to the Children of Yisra'el while they resided in the land of Horeb.

The wind calmed. The clouds waved overhead in grand formations as the Paraclete studied Moshe's overtures of prophecy – the presentation of Yehuway's Laws to the world. The clouds resembled a land mass while the blue sky appeared as an inverted ocean. Moshe wrote, "Children of Yisra'el. You personally carry within yourselves the undeniable witness of everything that Yehuway has performed in front of your eyes. Yes, who among you can ever deny what has taken place and the effects that those monumental things have had upon us as a nation and as a people? Tell your children and they, in turn, must tell their children, the true events that occurred in the land of Egypt. Read and understand what I have instructed my disciples to write.

"Parents, children, listen: you are the true witnesses of what Yehuway has performed against false leaders. Forever witness to the events of the final day of retribution so your children and their children may never forget the fires that fell from the clouds that held back the might of the armies, jets, ships who tried to murder you. Never extinguish from your memories the rush of the devouring locusts. Your words must forever recall the fleshly deformities that the Nations of the World suffered in their course of hatred against Yehuway, the true God of the Universe. Whenever you see a stream, a brook, or a river remember how the brown the river of all continents turned - a deep, blood red. Tell all the generations to come how an uncountable mob of frogs deafened the ears of the men encamped along the rivers and lakes and ponds – and how those unfiltered cries of the night forbade sleep and drove men and women and children insane. Yes, never forget the gigantic rise of the red, blue, and yellow circumference that carried on its weight a whirlwind topped by a mushroom of a hundred thousand lightning strikes—yes, a spectacular sphere of fire—that held back the jets and ships and armies of the variant nations. Yes, remember how in spite of that majestic terror, still the arrogant forces of the world flagrantly rushed headlong into the paths of the defending angels of righteousness until the very moment they unleashed their swords to forfeit the mighty wage naught.

"Let this thought strengthen in your minds: do not fear anguish of a retribution from the enemy's hand. Are they not dead? Those who did not learn the consequences of the historic defeat of their neighbors who warred against us, they will also perish. However, never forget the anguished looks of unbelieving surprise on the faces of the once arrogant and insolent soldiers as the power of Yehuway swallowed whole their tanks, their helicopter, their jets, their submarines, the battle destroyers, their atomic weapons, their infantry, their riflemen, and the terrorist. Who among them earned Yehuway's grace? Who among them called to the great God of Yisra'el to save him so he might repent and enjoin himself to our cause? What opposer admitted his folly and fell face down in humility and respect to our true and exclusive God?

"Only we—the believers in the righteousness of the children of Abraham, of Isaac, and of Yaakov—are permitted to carry the true witness of the great miracles that Yehuway performed on our behalf. Only our eyes will survive to the new day to declare to future generations what we saw. We will testify as a righteous nation that Yehuway raised a mighty army of extreme power to defend us against those who sought to annihilate us.

"Among all humanity," said the Paraclete, "I alone understand what is to occur. Today I will interpret it for you.

"I repeat: though you may be fortunate enough to live through the miracles of the coming day, Yehuway did not give you a reasoning heart to perceive what your eyes have seen until a generation after the last resurrected human being greeted his last offspring. Your intellect failed to grasp the significance of the events that forever affected you as an emerging nation from the consuming waters of the last battle from the edge of a filthy sea to the new shores of dignity. Today, all of you walk on the very same land that shall rise into an eternal nation – the sole and exclusive nation of the true and only God: Yehuway. Yes, your ears heard, but they failed to understand what they heard – yes, even to this very day.

"Listen now to Yehuway."

Yehuway's power spoke, "For thousands of years I protected human beings through the variant courses of hostility against you performed through the deceits of the demons. Through crag and valley, shadows and light, dry and wet, I protected you. During this time, not one single day passed where you went without the necessities of life. I, and I alone, assured you of your survival. Go ahead and examine yourself. Do you not yet breathe? Do you not still have your mothers and fathers features? When I dress you inside the tailors' shop who work in my Kingdom I will present to you threads as strong as steel. They will never rot. Your clothes will neither tear nor become frail. They will be without blemish. Not even a mere spot will linger on them. Examine for yourselves the shoes I will provide you to cover your feet. The leather will not thin. The straps will not frail. Moreover, on what day will any of you ever go hungry? Recall on the day of your realization of who I truly am, what was said about me in the prophecies, 'In order to survive, one must eat and drink, otherwise one will perish.' However, you have not eaten sweet bread. You have not drunk wine or any other type of strong drink. You who have been with me in spirit, thought, and action still survive. I alone have permitted your shoes and clothes to endure. It is I alone who has transformed your stomachs, blood, and liver to endure the treachery of your former bodies so you may know that I am Yehuway, your exclusive and only God. I alone raised from a humiliated race the world's most powerful military force. I am *'El Yehuway seba'ot*: the Raiser of Armies.

"After you have resided paradise for a bit, remember Sihon, the Amorite king of the city of Heshbon, and Og, the Amorite king of the city of Bashan who was a giant of a man—a Rephaim—who had united their military might and declared war against Me. They sought to destroy my believers, my faithful in total ruin, even after their leaders entreated you to pass unharmed through their lands in peace. The deceivers are powerful in their persuasion. I, alone, am able to slaughter all the opposers from the earth. Not one believer who adheres to me, will be permitted to fight against another human being for the battle of retribution is mine alone to execute. Do not arm yourselves! Do not sound out the war rally. To do so is to reflect your lack of belief in my ability to protect you. Yes, I, alone, will issue the war campaign's order to kill every man, woman, and child from the face of the earth who had fought against me. The lands that the opposers illegally dwelled upon I will present to the spiritual survivors on the evening of the last day of retribution. The land that the evil occupants occupied will became an eternal inheritance – just as I had promised to do so for Abraham.

"Impermanent is the consequence of the non-believers: occupiers but for a brief moment on the continents of the earth. Step aside those of you whom I can never recognize. It is better for the unrepentant not to have lived. My hand is set against you. In turn, I will bless those who leave peacefully for the sake of My purpose.

"In this manner I have kept my promise to the Children of Adam. Now, survivors, keep sacred in your own hearts the words of my covenant. Perform them diligently so you may prosper in everything that you do."

"Today I will make this covenant—this oath—not just with you, but also with those others who sit among you even though they may not be directly descendent from the loins of Abraham. I, Yehuway your true and only God, will also make this pledge with the person who is not yet born."

"I thus tell you now – it is better to destroy forever the most beautiful carving in the world if it is false, rather than admire its beauty even for one second for the filth that it truly represents. If there are any men or women or family or tribes whose heart turns away today from Yehuway our God to serve the gods of the nations that we have traversed through, there indeed exists a tinge of small seeds that will mature to produce poison weeds, gall, and wormwood.

"The sadness of gazing upon such beautiful things is more than their evil allure. A person who hears the words of philosophers and religionists can soon forget that their soothing sentences are but false words intermingled with truth. They are conniving in their betrayal. Their allure brings us into a world of evil. Everyone is subject to this fall. This occurs whenever the false person filled with succulent lies pretends to worship truth. The listener becomes enticed, and in that enticement leads himself toward a shameful curse.

"In exact contrast, Yehuway will bless those who turn toward him. Those persons may freely pronounce in truth and dignity these words in his heart, 'I will have peace.'

"Though the true in heart may pronounce themselves safe, the same cannot be said for the delusional man. He is a disguise even unto himself. He is a phony – a falsifier. Beware. He thinks: 'I will walk as my imagination dictates to me. My heart will embellish whatever image I desire to worship. I can get drunk to my satisfaction. My contentment is mine to achieve.' This sort builds fabulous marble edifices, not for My glory, but for his own vanity. Beware non-denominationalism! I hate your hypocrisy and your lies

"Yes, beware, because Yehuway will not spare the false man. Yehuway's anger compels His jealousy to rage passionately against that person.

"From the beginning of a person's birth every deed and thought is recorded and all the acts that had become harmful acts will return to afflict that person. Worse, Yehuway will blot out that person's name from under the stars of the heavens on the Day of Reckoning. How, then, can that person ever be resurrected? That person's name is forgotten in Yehuway's memory. When such happens, what mother, father, or brother, wife, husband, son, or daughter remembers that person? The vain builder of grand houses of worship and great governments and international enterprises will become an eternal forgottenness. His life a total absence. Do not mourn for such sinners – for those sinners have vanished, disappeared. More hollow than the tiniest of ashes.

"Such erasure is justified.

"Yehuway must separate the sinful person because the good community cannot accept an evil person's presence. The evil person will be disenfranchised from among all the continents of earth according to all the sanctions of the covenant that are written in the Book of the Law. Do not sin for the curse will be so profound, so conclusive, even the generation that will be born after that person's own children have died, will encounter a stranger from a far off land who will ask, 'How was it possible for the once good person to commit a crime against another? How, even after they have seen the plagues of that land and the sicknesses that Yehuway had laid upon it? Now, look, this entire land is nothing more than brimstone filled with salt. The land is a burning place. Utterly desolate. The land refuses to nourish any kind of seeds. Nothing can be produced on its surface. The land becomes identical to the lands of Sodom, Gomorrah, Admah, and Zeboim: the four regions that Yehuway overthrew in His time of anger and wrath.'

"Even all the nations will ask, 'Why did Yehuway do this to this land? How are we to interpret the depths of His great anger?'

"Other men will answer them with Yehuway's own words: 'Yehuway destroyed the lush beauty of the land because the Children of Adam forsook the covenant that they had pledged to Yehuway, the God of their fathers. Long ago, Yehuway concluded with them a Book of Laws after He rescued them from the lands of the Nephilim. They did not hold steadfast to the law. Instead, the people desired to worship the false and beautiful icons that permitted easy compromises. The Law became a mockery – a thing so remote and distant in their minds, even the simplest words became a complex image requiring disobedience. A "yes" became a "maybe." The "perhaps" a conclusive "yes" if it entangled wrong thoughts and actions. The firm "no" vanished as though the word had never held a meaning. The Children of Adam worshiped gods whom they knew not.'

"Did not Yehuway warn them against such a dire withdrawal of true worship from Him?

"Did they not witness the anger that Yehuway had kindled against this land to bring upon it all the curses that are written in the Book of Laws?

"As a farmer pulls out the bad weeds, Yehuway rooted the malicious people from the land allocated to them. Yehuway's dignity filled with wrath and indignation. He dispersed the ungrateful and insolent to utter chaos. The people trusted human ruler. The residents of those lands did not care to read and understand the laws of Yehuway because their fathers who originally worshiped correctly became lost in thought and, in turn, in identity. The realities of salvation they discarded.. However, the time is drawing near when Yehuway's reality can no longer be contained. This reality must now be revealed to so we may obey all the words of this law.

CHAPTER

3

THE PROPHECY, THE FORMER secret, is revealed. Shiloh emerges.

It will happen, when all the writings of Isaiah and Abishua (the fourth high priest of Israel in the line of Phinehas) are fulfilled and when the things spoken of by Jesus to his first cousin John the Apostle come true – then the fearful day will descend upon the unsuspecting. I tell you now: Jesus carries the same identity as Yehohshua. He is the Son of Yehuway. Never equal to, never to step into Yehuway's place, never to act as three-in-one, but the eternally obedient subject of his King Majesty, Yehuway. Jesus is Shiloh, unveiled.

Now, let Yehohshua speak for he is the same as Mikha'el the Archangel who is also known as "The Word of Yehuway". This is he who will carry the flaming sword atop a white war charger. This is the King and Priest – Melchizedek realized.

"True believers. My true anointed. The Paraclete now resides upon the earth. Finality is upon you. The earth's axis has shifted. The poles trade places. What was warm becomes cold. What was hot becomes mild. The mountains that you see here and there will, within a wink, be flattened and the dry land will blossom with vegetation and fig trees. Thus, adjust your personalities to accept what is to come because it comes for your benefit. What appears to be a frightful curse will transform to a blessing. The billions of lost lives will seem a curse, but the righteous among them will resurrect to life anew. The task of obedience that I now set before you, keep within your hearts to perform. Never forget the pronunciations of the Law of Righteousness. Glean from these Laws an unmistakable interpretation of My righteous indignation. Know and understand this thing: every person of every country will have a clear vision—a fantastical dream to some— why Yehuway (the God of all mankind who once drove the Children of Abraham out of the land He set aside exclusively for them then saw again to their return) dictates for the people of the earth to obey Him. All the nationalities of the earth, whether African, Asian, European, American, Hispanic, as well as the indigenous tribes of the earth, will return to Yehuway, the only true God of the Universe. Each person will obey Yehuway's voice according to everything that He has commanded to be performed. On that day henceforth, after the resurrection, all the children of the world, with uniform hearts and souls will worship the true God in unison, without differing policies. There will no longer exist a million religious discords or a hundred million political canvases – there will only be one."

Now, the Paraclete—directly inspired through the Holy Spirit—speaks.

"Do not think of the One uniting all to a singular thought with a universal language ever desired divisions and discords. Do not accept the thought that because Nimrod ruled a single group of people that the Father cursed the world because of their unification. The Father of all cursed Nimrod and those about because they had rebelled against the Father demanding man to rule man so they could wage war against the angels and Yehuway Himself. Black Nimrod thought himself supreme – a man who did not need to obey anything other than his own desires. So great was his arrogant hostility he dared to raise a tower, so his military machine could shoot arrows against righteous Yehuway. To counteract this hateful hunter without destroying the entirety of humankind, Yehuway mercifully confused the original Hebrew language into a multitude of languages. Was it not better that way? Was not Yehuway's tactic brilliant? Moreover, the political, language, monetary, cultural, and religious divisions will soon be over. Moneycracy has reigned and its brutality noted in the books of wrath. These false, hateful, unnecessary, and counter-productive divisions will stop. Original and righteous unification will come. One religion. One language. One society. One purpose. One monetary system: these are the righteous tasks of the True Provider. To think unification evil and malicious is to side with Satan."

Compassionate Yehuway

Listen, now, to the words of the Paraclete who is directly inspired through the Holy Spirit.

"On the Day of Finality, the day that Yehuway our Universal God turns our captivity away from the demons, Yehuway will have compassion on us. He will gather his great crowd—both Israeli and non-Israeli—from all the nations of the earth, yes, even from the remotest parts where Yehuway our God scattered the people to reside.

"The inhabited earth will consist of one fold, one flock. The children whom the Assyrians dispersed will remember their family's name. The children whom the

Romans cast aside and set adrift to reside in South Africa, and in Cochin in India, and in the faraway lands of China, will remember their family's name. The orphans as well as all the children born without a father's name will remember their birthrights."

"Everyone driven even to the outmost parts of the world will remember their family's name. Yehuway our God will gather us in front of His house. He, Himself, will fetch us back to live in our established homeland.

"Yehuway our God will return us to the land that our fathers once lived in. It is ours to possess. Yehuway is kind and generous. He will multiply our valuables above our fathers.

"Yehuway our God will circumcise our hearts toward righteousness. Even the depths of the body of our seed will learn to love Yehuway our God with all our heart, with all our soul. We will live in comfort and in peace.

"Yehuway, our true and only God, will put all His curses upon your enemies. However, never forget that it is the demons who influence the actions and thoughts of your enemies. Soon, though, the demons' hates and persecutions will cease to exist. The executioner's curse will lift. In turn, the demons will be eternally forgotten. The angry things that they caused will no longer be remembered. As for their instigator: the liar of liars, he will be locked up for a thousand years. During his imprisonment, you will learn truth and obeisance. You will see for yourselves how wonderful it is to obey the Laws of Yehuway. You will return to life from the pits of death so you will learn to obey the voice of Yehuway and to perform in righteousness all His commandments. Everything has been written in His Book of Laws. Today, it is made manifest in these new writings that are clarified and expanded upon. I have commanded the Paraclete to make it so this very day.

"Yehuway, our true and only God will make you plenteous in every work of your hand. It will be impossible for you to become bored or lazy in your pursuits, for everything will become the pleasure of the task maker. The health of your body will become strong and long lasting. The health of your livestock as well as the nourishment of your foods in the land of plenty will be good for everyone. Yehuway will again rejoice over you to perform for you good works just as He had rejoiced for your fathers.

"If you listen to the voice of Yehuway, our true and only God, and keep His commandments and His statutes that are written in this Book of the Law, and if you turn to Yehuway, our true and only God with all your heart and with all your soul, you, in turn, will enjoy prosperity and great happiness."

Yehuway now speaks through his only begotten son, Mikha'el the Archangel.

"Listen to me: The commandments that I am commanding you to perform are not hidden from you. Neither is the day far off when My son will reside upon his throne on the face of the earth in My capital, Jerusalem.

"Why are you surprised at this concept? That I, Yehuway, will soon establish My son upon a throne to rule in righteousness in the middle of Jerusalem sitting upon a gilded chair designed with motifs of grape vines and pomegranates? Have I not said it time after time that only My Son is the eternal ruler of man's affairs? Did I not say this when I spoke to Adam before he left the lush green lands of Eden? Did you not understand what I meant when I said to Adam, 'I shall put enmity between you and the woman, and between your offspring and hers. They shall strike at your head, and you shall strike at their heel'?

"What human can ask me: 'Who will You allow in heaven?'

"It is not for any human to say to another, 'Who among us will go to heaven? Who will bring down to us words of its wonders so we may hear about it? What must we do to reside in heaven?'

"I, Yehuway, I alone, invite whom I want to reside inside the rooms of My mansion. In it, I have built 144,000 rooms. I alone permit the occupiers to walk through my halls.

"'Where is Your Mansion?' someone dared to ask.

"It is neither in the sky, nor in the mountains. Neither is it beyond the sea, that you should say, 'Who is able to row over the sea for us and bring news of this wondrous Mansion, so we may walk through it ourselves to verify what we have heard about it? Who will perform this for us?'

"How is it that you cannot hear the word that is spoken in your ears? The words come to you in absolute truth, but you let the great truth linger about you as if it were nothing more than snowflakes. Yes, the depths of your ears fail to understand Me. I permit you to read what I have written; still you cannot understand what your own mouths have spoken! Please, I implore you: permit your hearts to examine what you have heard. Learn to listen to your own heart. Discern what has been published.

"Yet, somehow, an analysis of the heart and intellect fails to reach your mind. You have not discerned My words. They became a secret to you not because of Me – but because of yourselves. For six thousand years, I placed my words in front of your eyes. Are My words not reproduced in millions and millions of volumes in every country on the face of the earth?

"See, I propose to set before you on this very day a good and prosperous and healthy life. I am able to eternally vanquish death. I am a powerful God, strong enough to destroy all the evil things that cling to the earth. I can erase wickedness forever. Because of this, I can truthfully say and in fact, command you forevermore that you should love Yehuway, your true and only God. I have earned the right to ask all people to walk in My ways and to keep My commandments and My statutes and to listen to My judgments. Do this so you may live and so yours may multiply. I, Yehuway, your God, will bless you in the land that you will possess.

"However, if your heart turns away, so that you will not listen to Me, and you turn to other gods to serve them – I will henceforth denounce you. You will with absoluteness perish. You will not prolong your days upon the land where I led you. When you cross over the Jordan River to possess the land, remember it is I, Yehuway, who brought you to it."

Listen, now, to the words of the Paraclete who is directly inspired through the Holy Spirit.

"I call upon heaven and earth to record this day as a witness against you for your own behalf. Let today become an eternal witness of what has been declared. I set before you, life and death. Happiness and cursing. I implore you to choose life so you and your seed may remain alive.

"Live, so you may love Yehuway, our true and only God. Live, so you may obey His voice. Live, so you may cleave to Him, for he is your life as well as the length of your days. Live, so you may dwell in the land that Yehuway swore to your fathers to Abraham, to Isaac, to Yaakov.

"People of Gaza, listen to this final warning. Burn in your hearts Yehuway's own words for they will save the Palestians from the dictates of Hamas. They will save the Iranians from misguided mullahs. Hezbollah, rethink your tactics before you set an armed people where they should not go."

Yehuway speaks.

"The Land that I, Yehuway, gave to the Children of Abraham is an eternal gift. Those others, who chose to occupy that land, trespass against a most sacred oath. Leave the land while there is yet a day more to travel. Settle yourselves and your sons and daughters in a land that has not been set aside for My Children, and I promise you a wonderful blessing of prosperity and peace. Act in accordance with My desire so happiness and blessing and prosperity may come over all."

This is the Paraclete's petition to Yehuway to appoint his a world leader capable of dealing with the tragedies of modern civilization.

"Let Yehuway, the God of the spirits of all flesh, set a man over the congregations of the world. Let this man represent the people in true righteousness. Permit this man to enter the meeting hall to stand before the anointed Ruler of all with profound and designated representation. Let this man lead the people outside the regions of this land to cross the Jordan into a land set aside for true and righteous worship. Let this man be capable enough to bring the people to the region that had been set aside for them through a wondrous promise – a land to where these assembled people will raise their children in righteousness cradled in swaddling clothes of truth. A new people will originate in that land devoted exclusively to Yehuway. May this Congregation of Yehuway never become as mindless sheep without a shepherd.

"Yehuway, I ask for Your permission for that man to be chosen from among the people who stand before You. Let Your spirit traverse over them so from among them You may personally select Your anointed one. One to lead the people in delightful righteousness."

Therefore, listen again to the Paraclete who is directly inspired through the Holy Spirit. He implores, "Please, for our future's sake, do not permit a popular man to rise from among the populous. Do not permit an unrighteous man to lead. Do not permit anyone to obtain power who would dare to pronounce acts of glory in your name. Yehuway, you alone have the right to appoint a representative chosen through the divine instruction placed before us. Let all those who desire leadership to first verify through universal witness that You, Yehuway, appointed that man as a leader. Please anoint him in righteousness just as You had appointed Aharon and Moshe."

In the stress of night, the Paraclete implores a second request, "Do not permit a man to obtain representation through autocratic means. Yehuway, I acknowledge, leadership is established exclusively through Your personal appointments. Your own spirit guides man's hands. Endow that leader with wisdom in exercising judicial judgment."

CHAPTER

4

"BE STRONG. HAVE GOOD courage. Do not be afraid. Do not have any fear about the enemy who waits ahead. Yehuway, your God, travels with you. He will not fail you. He will not forsake you."

"Respect and honor Yehuway, our true and only God. Observe each word of the law so that when our children bear their own children, they may recount to them what they have learned. Remember, these coming generations will have never witnessed Yehuway's grandeur. They will doubt what they hear because they have not experienced what we ourselves have gone through. Teach our children to love and respect Yehuway our God. Do this so that as long as our children live in the land that we are about to settle, they will live in peace and in prosperity. After you have crossed the River Jordan, remember what I have spoken to you. Remember my final words in your hearts and minds. Yes, own them forever in your hearts."

"Yehuway is a warrior. His first created, Mikha'el the Archangel is a warrior prince. Yehuway is a God who raises armies. Everything that He does, He performs through rage and violence. The very creation was an act of violence against peaceful void."

"Yehuway confronted nothingness and from its dreaded terror brought forth life. "He ripped Void asunder so you might exist today. Tell me, was He wrong to want something to be from the depths of emptiness?"

"I am Yehuway who resonated the energies of creation throughout the universe.

"This I, Yehuway, pledge. Each place that the soles of the Fathers of the Children of Yisra'el walked upon, that land shall belong to the Nation of Yisra'el, just as I had spoken it to Moshe.

"From the southern Wilderness, to the entirety of Lebanon, even to the land where the southeastern Great River courses through: the river Euphrates. All the land that the Saudis now live in shall belong to the Nation of Yisra'el. Yes, even to the Mediterranean Sea from whose shores your people will eternally visit the setting of the sun. It shall belong exclusively to the children of Abraham, even to the western coast.

"Neither a single man nor a numerous army will be able to withstand Yehuway's onslaught. This will be true all the days of your life. As I was with Moshe so shall I walk with the eternal anointed. I am true. I, Yehuway, will neither fail nor forsake my believers or my faithful. Be strong! Courageous! I appoint My only begotten son to perform for the people the true and holy division of the land that shall become for them the eternal inheritance that I had sworn to their fathers to give them. To do this task, I only ask you to be strong as well as resolute, to observe faithfully everything according to the law which Moshe my servant commanded you to perform. Do not turn from my law neither to the right nor to the left. The law is perfect, as

I have presented it to you. It does not need superficial interpretations or deviations or supported and enhanced points of view. It is exactly what I meant it to be. Obey and listen to the laws that I have established so you may prosper wherever you go. Permit sensibility coupled with compassion to be your guide, for what I have given is a merciful gift that will transform the doomed human race into a blessed and elevated race of human beings.

"This Book of the Law must never depart from your lips. You must meditate, recite, and reflect day and night on what it teaches. Observe, perform, and abide by what is written in the book so you may prosper in your obedience to Me and succeed in your devotion toward Me. With these truths embedded in your heart and spirit, you will be able to flee from the ensnarement and entrapments of the falsehoods of the world: both religious and political. I have nothing to do with the vain constructs of glittering stages nor do I bless or consider the petitions of the men and women who stand before their podiums speaking betraying words that will only result in your damnation and death.

"Thus, in order to protect you from the malicious profiteers who intend their wicked desires to mislead and harm you, I must command that each man wear My words upon his forehead so you may always be strong with a resolve of great courage. Do not be afraid. Neither be dismayed. I, Yehuway, am your true and only God. Wherever you go, I will be with you."

"Yehuway asks: 'Will you obey Me and observe My decrees. Will you keep Me always in front of your eyes as your only true God?'

"I am Yehuway, your only true God. I am He who will provide to you salvation from the greed of nations who strive to thwart you into their created House of Bondage which is ruled by satanic influence. Due to Adam's transgression you had resided as an afflicted race of hated aliens. Because I, Myself, will deliver you from your stressful suffering and harsh labors and freed you from those scornful and prejudiced countries, you shall have no other gods before Me.

"I have long ago earned your allegiance.

False Images

"You must not make for yourselves any sort of sculptured image of any sort of animal: fish, lion, bear, or eagle as a symbolic representation of power and purpose for yourselves. Nor should you carve or paint images of men and women. Any sort of symbol that represents anything on the face of the earth or in the heavens must never be fashioned as a keepsake or as a memory of what once lived. A bull is nothing more than a bull as a sheep is nothing more than a sheep. A strong man is nothing more than a man temporarily alive just as the weak man is alive. A beautiful woman in your eyes is nothing more than a being clothed in flesh no more deserving of being loved by Me than a woman whom you may scorn and view as less than desirable. Flesh is nothing more than flesh. Flesh is temporary. Do not record it. Do not sculpture it. Do not paint it. Flesh is dust and withers away to blow in the wind. The maggots that I have already sent forward consume all flesh.

"I alone am eternal. I am an impassioned God. For My passion, I will one day release the guilt's burden that

Adam and Havva brought upon their children. For their disobedience, today, you walk within Adam's failures. Nevertheless, I have created a plan of restitution that will satisfy their debt against Me.

"Never bow down toward any man, no matter what his prestige may seem to you. There is only one ruler over the affairs of humankind, and that singular ruler is Myself. I am Yehuway, the exclusively God of the Universe. Never enslave yourself to other men, for who are they, but temporary things existing in a temporary society filled to the rim with temporary actions? I will show tender mercy even up to one thousand generations. My tenderness will give rise to a generation of pure souls who will emerge from the dung heaps of enslavement. Yes, those who will rise to live in purity are today an unknown group of people. I assure you, however, that from the very genes of those who are alive today will be born a people of spiritual purity. These purified people, I shall present as a gift to the other races of mankind on the 7,000th year of the creation of Adam. These pure in heart will forever obey My commandments. Every day they will practice compassionate love, inspired by an inextinguishable desire to help all the races of humankind. I will establish them as the leaders and educators of those who shall be reborn from death into an existence of spiritual purity. This will be their second chance to live in a world of enlightenment without strife or conflict or jealousy.

False Usage of Yehuway's Name

"You must not make any type of pledge to another using My sacred name as though I am your witness of a testified act. You must never use My name under false

52

pretenses as an act to validate a business contract. Do not use My name as a testimony to an event that you have sworn to perform. These are private matters between yourself and yourself, and between yourself and family members, or between yourself and others. Such matters of business or family relations or testimonies of events are not My concern. Do not involve Me as a witness for your cause, for what I deem to perform, I alone shall perform it. I alone bear My own testimony.

"Remember, each and every Saturday is a holy day set aside by Me as a gift to mankind so human beings may respect Me and have a brief interval of time for relaxation from their weekly tasks. Reflect amidst this day of calm. Work for six days, then on the seventh day you, your daughter, your son, your servants, your cattle, and even the foreign residents and travelers who happen to visit within the lands governed by My laws, shall all rest from their burdens. I worked for six spans of time to create the earth and the heavens and all the living things on the land and in the depths of the ocean. Hallowed is the seventh span of time.

Yehuway's universal commandments

"Honor your father and your mother so you may long endure within the lands that I have personally set aside for you.

"You must not murder.

"You must not commit adultery.

"You must not steal.

"You must not bear false testimony against your neighbor.

"You must not jealously covet your neighbor's house or his possessions. What he has established for himself, belongs to him. Rather, be happy for the possessions he has accumulated or inherited. Perhaps in your genuine joy for his prosperity, he may share with you or with your family portions of his own riches. Do not forget that all things are temporary. Gold, silver, furnishings, even the mountains, and the oceans, and the clouds, as well as the clothes, and the fruits, and the bread, and the meat are temporary. Your very lives are temporary, until the coming era of your entrance into eternity through the salvation of My own loving benevolence. If you do not prosper in this temporal world as you may believe you should, what concern should it be to you? Will you not one day rise to enjoy new life with a permanently healthy body? In the new era to come, in the foundations of My Kingdom, build for yourself a strong house with thick stones. With an eternal and superior intellect, learn the skills of the great carpenter. Build for yourselves beautiful possessions. Till your own land and plant for yourself whatever fruits and vegetables you desire.

"You must not desire your neighbor's wife. Her beauty and cunning will wither. Through the years, what remains but wrinkles and a faint heart? To prefer the love of your neighbor's wife may lead you to lose My love.

"Do not persuade from your neighbor his choice helpers so they may work for you. Leave your neighbor's male and female servants alone.

"Do not steal your neighbor's ox, or his best donkey, or anything else that may belong to your neighbor."

"Do not fashion or manufacture gods from gold or silver or wood. An earthen altar is all that I require. Atop it, perform your burnt sacrifices of sheep and oxen. I will see it. With its sincere performance, I will bless you.

"If you build me an altar from a group of stones, do so with only the very rocks that are strewn over the plains. Do not labor to fashion the stones or smooth them or shape them. What exists as is, is good. The tools that touch the stones blemish the stones.

"Never build steps to reach a raised altar. I do not desire to see your naked ass or your exposed penis as your clothes lift from your body as you climb the steps. The entire altar is sacred to Me and to Me alone. From its depths I see everything as well as from the heights above it.

ଓଓଓଓଓଓଓ

Edict Against Slavery

"These now are the judicial prescriptions which you must set before yourselves.

"If you happen to have had forced a person into servitude you must free that person. That person shall go free and without compensation to you and without further obligations to your needs or desires for additional labor or counseling. If it happened that the person was married when the person became your indentured slave, the person's spouse must also leave your service.

"Remember that it was I who presented Adam with a wife, and the sons and daughters that were born through that union, became Mine to provide for to love and to nourish and to help flourish in the wonders and mercy of My law.

"No person shall be a slave to another.

Treatment of Wives & Virgins

"Concerning multiple wives of false religions. To align yourself with my purpose, have only one wife.

"If it should happen that a father arranges for his daughter to become a wife and if she displeases her husband who had betrothed her, he must permit her to re-purchase her freedom so she may return to either her prior house, or establish herself in her own house with her own possessions.

"If it happens that a purchaser deceitfully coerced a marriage with false intents, the husband forfeits his ability to keep her entrapped in his house, or any of his relative's house, or friend's house as a forced companion. He, or any of his relatives, or friends, will not have any power over her as he himself dealt deceitfully with her.

"Moreover, if the purchaser of a maidservant betroths her to his own son, he shall deal with her after the manner of his own daughters born to him through his own loins.

"If a man purchases a maidservant as a second or a third wife or more, he must continuously treat her as a proper wife with all the rights and tributes allocated to such a person. He may not refuse to provide her with food, or clothing, or sexual responsibilities, or educational advances. Under no circumstances may anyone diminish a female's capacity as a human being. She has the full rights of a human being: respect, dignity, possessions, education, with the rights of approaching her husband and children as a caretaker and as an advisor to the family's welfare. Her breasts and lack of a penis do not make her as an inferior being. The secondary position assigned to her resulted from Havva's asking—through the satanic and seductive and manipulative whispers—for Adam to also sin against Me, but in the eyes of man, she is not to be treated as a whore unworthy of salvation. Love is the recompense. If the man fails his woman in these three areas of responsibility, then she has the absolute right to obtain her freedom without payment.

It is better to have one wife, faithful to God first.

"When a man entices a virgin who is not betrothed to perform sexual intercourse, he must surely endow her to be his wife. If her father utterly refuses to give her to him, the violator of her chastity must pay whatever money the father demands according to the dowry of virgins."

Murder & Accidental Death

"Prior to Yehohshua's fleshly appearance on earth the commandment uttered to Moshe was this: 'Should it occur that a person fatally strikes another person, that person shall surely be put to death. If by circumstance and unforeseen accident another person kills another person, place that accidental death into the hands of God. God will appoint a place of refuge for such a happenstance.

" 'However, if a person, with premeditated action, murders his or her neighbor or acts against his neighbor with treachery and deceit, then the judges and lawyers, who are the protectors of the land, must take that person from My altar and pass judgment against them to be punished to death.'

"After my son's ransom sacrifice on the cypress beam, I am allocating a grace period of mercy for the injured to enact within the prior commandments, mercy. Plead for the offender so your own wrongs may be forgiven you. On judgment day, I, alone, will kill the murderer if the heart remains cruel."

" 'The person who strikes his or her father or his or her mother shall surely be put to death. The person who insults his or her father or his or her mother shall suffer the death penalty. It is the same as hating Me for having created you from the elements of the earth on which you now reside: an earth filled with food and water and joyful possibilities.

"This pertains to ISIS, HAMAS, the Somalians, and any other practicer of evil intents to abuse other human beings. The person who kidnaps another person, whether or not that person sells or keeps the stolen one, that person shall surely be put to death. No nation must leave ISIS or the Somalians at peace. On judgment day, I will kill the enslaver.

"If a terrorist murders other persons at airports, subway stations, shopping malls, airplanes, trains, buses, or in any place of gathering, that terrorist will suffer eternal damnation, his name erased perpetually from My memory. On judgement day I will kill the terrorist.

"If a person argues with another person, and in the fury of that argument strikes the other with a stone or with his fist, but he does not perish as a result of the blow, and the injured person is rendered to his bed to recuperate, the striker will not be punished if the struck person rises again. Even if that blow upon the injured person cripples him so he must forever walk with a cane, the one who struck the injured person will only be required to compensate the victim for the loss of his or her lost time until thoroughly healed.

"If a person strikes the disposed, whether a male or a female prisoner, with a rod and he or she dies under that person's hand, that striker must ask for mercy from the injured person's relatives. However, if the offender fails to ask for forgiveness, on judgment day, I, alone, will judge the offender if the heart remains cruel."

"You have heard it said that 'If a person injures another, even though that person is a servant or free-person, that person shall suffer an identical punishment' but after my son's ransom sacrifice on the cypress beam, I, alone, am capable of judging the offender on judgment day."

"If it occurs that men engage in a battle amongst themselves and one should happen to push another against a pregnant woman and a miscarriage results, but without further sufferings, the responsible man must beg forgiveness from both the husband and the offender must make monetary compensation to the wife and husband to make amends to the injured. The courts will enforce the payments that the judges determine.

"After my son's ransom sacrifice on the cypress beam, I am allocating a grace period of mercy for the injured to enact within the prior commandments, mercy. Plead for the offender so your own wrongs may be forgiven you. On judgment day, I, alone, will avenge the offender if the heart remains cruel."

"You have heard it said from Moshe, 'if any damage does occur to the fetus or to the woman, the courts must enforce equal restitutions: a life for a life; an eye for an eye; a tooth for a tooth; a hand for a hand; a foot for a foot; a burn for a burn. Yes, an exact wound for an exact wound, and a bruise for a bruise' however, the strict adherence to this decree to equate sin for sin until the time approaches for the coming of the ultimate law performer is now set aside for the redeemer has come to the earth in the form of flesh and will redeem you from your burdens. The fulfiller of the law, the Ultimate Mashi'ach: the Mashi'ach of Mashi'achs, has appeared. On judgment day, I, Yehuway, will avenge the offender if the heart remains cruel."

"You have heard it said from Moshe, 'If it happens that a person strikes the eye of their slave, whether a male or a female, and either one of them becomes blind as a result of that blow, the owner of that slave must present to their slave their freedom for the sake of the destroyed eye. If the owner knocks out the male or female slave's tooth, the owner must release either slave because of the damaged tooth, however, the fulfiller of the law, the Ultimate Mashi'ach: the Mashi'ach of Mashi'achs, has appeared. On judgment day, I, Yehuway, will avenge the offender if the heart remains cruel."

"If it happens that an angry person murders either a man or a woman, on Judgement day I will avenge the harmed person.

"If it discovered that the parents of the angry person performed a lack of judicial training, I will directly take vengeance of the harmed person on Judgement Day.

"Both the angry person and the parents shall be held accountable for their decisions.

"If a criminal remains a recurring problem, and the courts place a fine against the criminal and the guilty person remains unrepentant, the parents must be brought to court to stand trial for their offsprings' crimes.

"Satan in the battle between good and evil and does not distinguish between parent and child, neither shall I.

Purposeful Harm

"If it happens that a person digs a hole in the ground and leaves the pit uncovered or fails to fill it back with dirt, and a person, ox or a donkey falls into the hole, the digger of the pit must compensate the hurt person or see to the animals safe recovery. The dead beast will become the property of the digger. If a person's animal should happen to hurt another person's animal and it perishes; both persons shall together sell the living animal. Together they must then divide the money from the sale as well dig the grave for the carcass of the dead animal.

Animal Abuse

"However, if the owner owns a bull which has a reputation for goring others in times past, and the owner deliberately failed to contain the dangerous animal, the owner must surely restore ox for ox. The dead ox, in turn, will become the offender's property as a life for death.

"If a thief steals an ox or a sheep and kills it or sells it, he shall restore five oxen for an ox and four sheep for a sheep. If the owner catches the thief while performing the crime in the depths of the darkness in the night as he is burrowing his hole and should it occur in his haste to escape that the tunnel collapses on him, or if he should suffocate or be crushed to death, no blood-vengeance shall be shed for him. The same shall apply if the stolen animal suffers death in the crevice of the tunnel. If, however, the sun has already risen and the owner catches the theft during the daytime, and the owner kills the thief in a rage of vengeance, then the murderer shall suffer punishment for killing the thief. The same shall apply if a witness testifies against a thief that the thief killed a once living animal. The caught thief must make full restitution. If the thief has nothing to pay as restitution, then the thief will forfeit his freedom and suffer enslavement until the debt is paid. If the stolen animal by the thief is found yet breathing, whether an ox or a donkey or a sheep; the thief must repay double its value.

"If a person permits his livestock to graze in another owner's field or vineyard so the produce is eaten to the very roots, the owner of the livestock must pay the owner of the field everything that is due him, even unto full value of the crops.

"When a person asks their neighbor to protect their donkey, or an ox, or a sheep, or any other sort of beast and it dies or becomes hurt, or is driven away, the matter must appear before the courts. If no one can provide a good accounting for the death or injury of the animal, then a sworn oath of non-intentional harm in front of Yehuway's representatives and between the two parties shall suffice. The owner of the discarded or displaced items must accept the verdict of innocence. The safe-keeper is not required to make restitution. However, if indeed the safe-keeper admits that a theft of the property occurred, he shall make restitution to the original owner.

"If an animal entrusted to the safe-keeper is torn to pieces by a predator beast: a lion, a leopard, a hyena, or a vicious animal, then let the safe-keeper bring the carcass of the destroyed animal as a witness so the marks of the predator may be testified to. In such a case, the safe-keeper does not need to make compensation for it.

"If a person determines to borrow an animal from his or her neighbor and should it happen to become injured or dies, the owner must receive due compensation. If it happened that the original owner was present with the animal when it sustained its injury or death, the borrower does not have to compensate the owner as the owner himself failed to protect that which he already owned. However, if the renter rented the animal to perform a task, and the animal sustained an injury or death, the owner must nevertheless receive his payment for the animal's hire, even though the task was not completed. Why tarnish a man's good intents as a deliberate malediction when outside and unforeseen intrusions may possibly interfere with life's events?

"If by chance you happen to discover your enemy's ox or his donkey going astray, surely you must return it back to him. Also, if by circumstance, you happen to see the owner's donkey (yes, even though that person may hate you or you hate that person) suffering under a heavy burden, help that person raise the donkey back on its feet.

"Do not eat any meat torn by lions, leopards, and hyenas that roam the fields. Throw away this mangled and brutalized meat for the bellies of the scavenger dogs, for they are already an unclean and filthy animal. They are the vomit and shit eaters of this world.

Deliberate Fires

"If by chance and circumstance a fire breaks out and the fire enflames the thorns so that stacks of grain or bags of grain, or anything remaining alive in the field is consumed with the fire's wrath, the person who ignited the flame must make restitution.

Pilferage & Abuse of a Workman's Tools

"If a person presents to another person their money or produce or products, or materials, or tools, or anything of value to protect it, and the items happen to be stolen from the safe-keeper's possession, and if the thief is discovered with the merchandise, let him become the one who pays double its value. If, however, the thief is not found, then the master of the house shall be brought before the judges to see whether or not he had placed his or her goods in proper safe-keeping for full guarding of the neighbor's goods. In all manners of distrust, trespass, and pilfering, whether it is for an ox, a donkey, a sheep, or for clothing, or for any other sort of lost items, when a challenge appears before the courts, the causes of both parties shall come before the judges. The judges alone shall condemn the guilty. Thereafter, when the verdict is established, the guilty person shall pay double to his neighbor the displaced properties.

ଓଷ୍ଠଓଷ୍ଠଓଷ୍ଠଓଷ୍ଠଓଷ

Witches, False Prophets, False Gods

"You must not tolerate a witch to live among you. The false prophet must be removed from the city to live in an isolated place where he cannot be heard. The false preacher and practicer of magical spells are aligned with the demons.

"I speak of soothsayers, tarot card readers, palm hand readers, shape of skull readers, astrological diviners, preachers on the pulpit who prophesy falsely.

"The person who worships any god, save Yehuway alone, shall be utterly destroyed on the Judgement Day.

"Beware the false writers who create fiction of wizards who associate with other wizards filled with images of dragons. The literature is incendiary to me.

"'Do not consider the entreaties of those who claim to be acquainted with the spirits of the dead or who chant for magical and mysterious things to encompass you as a veil of protection and enrichment or to place an adversary at bay. The chants and spirits defile you. I alone am the true God. I am Yehuway your exclusive God.

"Speak to the Children of Yisra'el. Say to them, "I am Yehuway your God. DO not perform enchantments, nor observe the seasons of times as a magical intercessor. The stars rotate as they do because I alone caused the cycles. What is it to Me to shift their orbits or to obliterate them? It is nothing."

"Do not revile God, nor curse Me because I am He who alone rules over all humanity. What power, what words can a person utter against divinity? What manner of fright may a false person instill in a just and worthy representative?

"Never set aside or delay the task of offering to Me the first ripe fruits. Do not take for yourselves what first emerges from the shaft of the tree or the womb of the animal. The firstborn of all things belongs exclusively to Me. I alone endowed all living and existing things with the first breath of life. The tops of the liquors are Mine as are the firstborn of your sons. The best of everything, in complete totality, you should present to Me with a loving spirit. Perform the same rendering of the first fruits of your oxen as well as your sheep. The concerns and necessities of the world that permit you to survive against the elements and treachery concern Me more so. Follow this formula: for seven days the firstborn sheep and goat and cow and the doves and birds that you keep among yourselves as well as the first fruits will remain with the birthing mother so they may be nourished and strengthened. Then on the eighth day you will present the strong and healthy gift to Me. In return, I will entrust My own firstborn to you so he may eradicate the filthy sin that resides everywhere among you. An equal balance shall take effect, for the heel that was injured in the days of Adam shall be recompensed to Me.

"I have established these sets of guides and procedures so you may become a holy people to Me and survive My day of hatred against the evil persons.

Protect the Foreign Visitor

"You must never wrong a person who is traveling through your land or mistreat the foreigner, nor oppress that person.

"You should never afflict any widow or a fatherless child. If you afflict them in any manner, I will hear their outcry to Me on the very instance of your treachery against them. My wrath shall blaze against the perpetrator. I will kill the offender with the sickle-sword on the Judgement Day.

Usury

"If you lend money to any of My people who are poor among you, you must not act toward them as an abusive lender. Do not demand usury. The loan, for mercy's sake of presenting life anew, is enough compensation.

"If you take your neighbor's raiment as a pledge, you must return it to him or her before the sun goes down. It is their only clothing: the sole garment for their skin against the elements of the world. How will they be able to sleep without the warmth and protection of their wool garment?

"When that cold and shivering person cries out to Me, I will hear their voices. Unlike yourselves, I am gracious toward the poor. While the world sleeps in mists of forgotten dreams, I think of the impoverished. I have developed a plan of salvation for them. Align yourselves toward My salvation for all mankind.

False rumors concerning others

"Do not stir the hearts of your companions with a false report against other men and women. Do not falsify or spread lies and unwarranted rumors created through a jealous or misinformed heart. Do not place yourself in the hands of a wicked person or try to persuade such a lowly one to act as an unrighteous witness for your false deeds. Never permit yourself to take sides with a multitude to do evil acts against an innocent person. Neither should you defend an unworthy cause so it may turn against the true and honest judgment. To pervert truth is to pervert holiness.

Neither must you contradict a poor man in his cause. Righteousness is not exclusive to the wealthy.

Do not influence others

"You must not seek to influence the rights and thoughts of the poor people who live among you in order to gain for yourself an unreasonable law to justify a selfish cause. I alone present to humanity a cause worth dying for.

"Distance yourself from false matters. Do not kill an innocent person because he has spoken absolute truths to you, regardless of the painful revelations those truths manifest to all listeners. I cannot justify wickedness. What wicked and evil act ever makes wrong right?

Refuse Bribes

"Never accept bribes. A bribe blinds the wise and perverts the words of the righteous.

"Never oppress the foreigner who travels through your land. You do not know the heart nor the character of the alien resident or visitor.

"Be circumspect with everything that I have said to you. Never mention the names of other gods, neither let their names be heard out of your mouth."

CHAPTER

5

YEHUWAY CONTINUED SPEAKING THROUGH his foremost representative Mikha'el the Archangel.

Sacred Saturday, The True Sabbath Day

"Every week of every year keep sacred the Sabbath—the Holy Saturday—to Yehuway. For six years, you will sow your field, and for six years, you will prune your vineyard to gather to yourselves the fruits. However, the seventh year shall become a Sabbath—as though it were a Holy Saturday—for the land to rest. You will neither sow your field, nor prune your vineyard. Whatever grows of its own accord, do not harvest it. Do not collect the grapes of the vines. Leave the fields undressed, for it is a year of rest for the land. Practice judicial crop rotation and conservation methods.

"However, whatever grows on its own accord on that land during its Sabbath span let your friends and visitors as well as the hired laborers who live with you as well as your cattle and the beasts of the field eat whatever they desire from the land's yields. Share with all what is freely given.

"Maintain the practice of the Sabbath for the sake of your land. Treat it as though the land were enjoying its own private Sabbath—a Holy Saturday—throughout the year. It shall mean for you invigorated crops, produce, and an abundance of fruit trees for you and for your servant as well as for your maid and your hired servant. Yes, the invigorated and energized land benefits you as well as the stranger who sojourns with you. Even your cattle and the beasts that are in your land shall all benefit and increase. Enjoy in the eighth year the fattened and luxuriant meat.

Feast of Unleavened Bread

"Maintain the Feast of Unleavened Bread. For seven days you will eat unleavened bread, as I had commanded you during the month Abib. On the fifteenth day of the same month is the feast of unleavened bread to Yehuway. Do this in the month of Abib because in that month you gained your freedom from enslavement from Egypt as an afflicted race of aliens. In the first day of the feast, you shall not perform any servile work. It is not necessary to pledge a holy convocation to that effect. Rather, offer an offering on the Altar of Fire to Yehuway. Perform this each day for seven days, and then on the seventh day, make it again as the first day: a day set aside for a holy convocation. Perform no servile work therein. Remember, not one resident is permitted to stand before Me with an empty stomach as it may foster a remorseful heart among the poor against Me.

"All who emerge from the darkness of the womb to the light of life become Mine. Every firstling born to your cattle, whether an ox or a sheep, if it is a male, it belongs to Me. However, there is this exception: the firstling of a donkey you must instead redeem with the life of a lamb. If you are unable to redeem him with the life of a lamb, then you must break his neck. All the firstborn of your sons you will also redeem.

"None shall approach My altar without first making a sacrifice of the choicest first born animal: sheep, goat, turtle dove, the first and premium wheat grains or fruits. Do not appear before Me empty-handed as I am going to present to you My own first born to redeem you from the chains of sin.

"Six days you will work, but on the seventh day you will rest. Whether it is during the time of shearing or in the season of the harvest – you will rest.

Feast of the Harvest

"Also, celebrate the Feast of the Harvest. Gather from the fields and the fruit trees the first-fruits of the wheat harvest, and the Feast of Ingathering at year's end when you have gathered the results of your labors in the field. During this feast, celebrate the victory of the first fruits emerging from the stress of your labors that you have sown in the field.

"Moreover, you must number seven weeks of year—forty-nine years—seven times seven years. During the tenth day of the seventh month, on the Day of Atonement, you must sound out the Trumpet of the Jubilee throughout your land.

Jubilee

"Proclaim the fiftieth year as a sacred span of time. Proclaim liberty throughout all the land for all the inhabitants who live therein. The fiftieth year must become a celebration for you. Yes, a jubilee. During this hallowed span, each man who had left his home to go abroad, must return to his own house and to his own family. A jubilee shall that fiftieth year be for you. You shall not sow; neither reap, that which grows by itself, nor gather the grapes from your vineyard. Leave the fruits undressed. For this is the time of the jubilee. It must be a holy span of time for you. You may only eat the things that grow on their own accord in the fields. Do not fear for your hunger. I will pollinate the trees and the vegetables and invigorate the land for your sakes.

"In the year of the jubilee each of you must return to where you were raised or to where you once held possessions. Seek out the allocated home of your ancestors. If through circumstances of one type or another you sold your property to your neighbor, or bought a piece of land from your neighbor, you must not commit anything offensive against each other. According to the number of years after the jubilee, you may repurchase what was once yours from your neighbor. And, according to the number of years of the bearing fruit trees, he is permitted to sell it back to you. And, according to the multitude of years you nourished the land, you may increase the land's price. It would be better, however, if you are able to diminish the price of the property according to the number of years that the fruit trees were able to make profits for you. It would behoove you to sell what you had purchased from the original owner back to the original owner after subtracting the amount of profits that his land permitted you to gain.

"To maintain fairness with suitable obligation, you must never oppress each other. Neighbor looks after neighbor so all neighbors may be fair to each other. Obey this inheritance law. Render through respect for

Me an allocation of justice among each other, for I am Yehuway your God who deals fairly and considerately with you.

"Therefore, perform My statutes and keep My judgments. Do them and you shall dwell in the land in safety.

"The land shall yield her fruit, and you shall eat your fill, and dwell therein in safety. If you say, 'What shall we eat during the seventh year? Look! We did not sow nor have we gathered what has been so abundantly provided to us!' Then listen to My words. I will command My blessing to come upon you during the sixth year. My power will bring forth fruit for three years. In turn, you will sow during the eighth year and eat that produce and crops. Store and preserve the past year's remainder of fruit and vegetables until the ninth year. Consume what you have until the fruits of the new harvest produce for your new growths. Yes, eat from what has been set aside in your storage houses and bins.

"In truth, the land may never be perpetually sold to another because the land belongs to Me. It is Mine. Remember, you are the foreign residents and sojourners who had traveled with Me to this land. Therefore, throughout the lands which are in your possession, you shall grant redemption for the land during the times that I call for it to be performed.

"Three times during the year all your males shall appear before your Sovereign Lord Yehuway. You must never offer to Me the blood of the sacrificial animal with leavened bread. Neither shall the fat of the sacrificial animal that is presented to Me remain until the morning. The first of the first fruits of your land you must bring into the House of Yehuway: your exclusive God.

"You must never seethe a kid in his mother's milk."

Mikha'el the Archangel

Yehuway said, "Behold, look upon the Archangel who stands before you speaking My words to you. His name is Mikha'el the Archangel. It is this very same angel who walked with the Children of Yisra'el from Egypt and across the Sea of Reeds, and into the battlefields against the Amalekites and against Og. Throughout eternity he will walk among the righteous to help them persevere in the laws that I have established for them.

"Mikha'el the Archangel is My firstborn. He is the ultimate redeemer for your sins. He alone will bring you to the place that I have prepared for you. Yes, because he is My son and the ultimate preserver of mankind, respect him with all your heart and soul. Conduct yourselves with full dignity so you may gain favoritism in his eyes to preserve you from falling into disgrace and unredeemable sin. Obey his voice. Do not provoke him, for he will not pardon your transgressions. Mikha'el the Archangel is my firstborn. My only son who was taken directly from My own energy. On earth as in the heavens Mikha'el the Archangel shall eternally be entitled: The sole and exclusive heir and representative of My name. He bears all My ingredients within his personality. He is the most highly favored among all My creations.

"Indeed, if you obey his voice and perform everything that I have instructed him to repeat to you; then I will become an enemy against your enemies and an adversary to your adversaries. My Angel shall walk ahead of you. He will lead in victorious battle against the Iranians, the Syrians, the Lebanese, the Egyptians, The Saudis, ISIS, the Taliban, Hezbollah, and all others who will try to war against My Holy Nation."

With the strongest voice anyone ever heard, Mikha'el the Archangel, in unison with his Creator's voice shouted: "I WILL ANNILATE ALL WHO WAR AGAINST THE CHILDREN OF YISRA'EL!"

Mikha'el the Archangel, in his perpetual role as spokesman between mankind and his Creator, returned to his recitation.

"You must never bow down to the false gods of the nations and local villages that surround you. Never serve them. Never perform the things that they perform. Never follow the least of their practices. Annihilate and destroy the false occupiers that inhabit the land that we will be entering. You, yourselves, must take this responsibility into your own hands as the battle between the unrighteous and the righteous is yours to bear, just as it has always been mine to bear. This alliance began with Seth and carried onward through No'ah then to Shem then to Eber: the father of all Hebrews. From Eber, the testimony carried to Abraham, whom I met on the road outside the city of Ur. As I wrestled with Yaakov, I will wrestle with the arrogant in heart. I will war against the nations of unrighteousness. Therefore, pulverize to the smallest fragment all the images of all the false gods. Destroy the statues, burn the paintings and the carved woods, dismantle and crush the stones of their buildings. The Pyramids, the Sphinx, the glorified reliefs, the representations carved into the mountains and inside the deepest caverns must be totally destroyed. What has been preserved and valued as art forms, are hideous in the sight of Yehuway, the only true and exclusive God of the Universe. The grandest churches of all religions, without exception, even the most fabulously enriched marbled edifices, even the adorned mosaics, wondrous to the human eyes, as well as all the pillars in all lands of the earth—again, without exception—bring to utter ruin. If you cannot bring yourselves to destroy them, do not fret, nor mourn, nor long for their return after I, myself, destroy them.

"Yehuway will instruct you on new designs acceptable to Him for your houses of worship. This will occur after the mighty tribulation: the Great Armageddon.

"You must serve Yehuway, your one and only God. In turn, He will bless your bread and your water. He alone is capable of saying: 'I will take sickness away from the midst of you. Not a single mother will suffer a miscarriage or bear terrible pain when she gives birth to her child. The parents will instruct that child, leading it to the worship of the only true God: Yehuway.

"Indoctrinate truths in your child's heart and mind before the indoctrination of evil overcomes your child. What is set cannot be corrupted. Do this, parents, so all the days of your lives will become enjoyable and fulfilling.

"Listen to the words of the Great Creator: the First and only Entity of the Universe. There is none beside the Father of All. In turn, the Father permits me to walk among you as your protector and as your encourager to achieve victories against your enemies. Therefore, guard your conscience so you may wake as a purified person with a life filled with goodness and justice. In turn, the Father permits me to send forth my fear before you. I will destroy all the people who war against you. I will create confusion and dread in the camps of all of your enemies and they will race away from you so that all you will ever see is their backs running away. I will indeed make all your enemies turn tail before you. I will send hornets and cause the people to suffer a great depression on account of your strength. A submissive dejection will fill their hearts and bodies with the ills and calamities of the earth. Their consciousness will be overwhelmed with distress. They will whine with tears of remorse. Through your righteous devotion to the Creator, I will drive out the Hivites, the Canaanites, and the Hittites who now falsely and arrogantly occupy this land. As long as you maintain the hopes and aspirations of a nation of people devoted singularly to the true God, so will I remain beside you. Do not risk yourselves to abandon your devotion toward righteousness, for I in turn, may equally abandon you. Do not become like the villagers and towns-people surrounding you. With a false boast they say to the world, 'Our fathers came to this land and they broke the ground to till it to bear fruits. Our children were born into this land. In our houses, our wives cook our meals and sew our garments. This land is ours.' However, I say this to the false occupiers: What god on what earth determined for you to live in the sacred land? Only the false vanity and the words of the terrible and loathsome enemy of Yehuway impregnate your minds. Walk away from what does not belong to you rather than die an eternally forgotten death. Who then will remember you or your wives or your children or your houses?

"Children of Earth, take this into account, for I know you have great expectations of how quickly you will come to occupy the lands promised to Abraham: the victory will come bit by bit, gradually, over a long span of time. Those present will die as well as their children and children's children. Know this absolute truth: This land will become the fully established nation of Yisra'el. This land is set side first for the righteous one, then from its capital, it will rule the world. But I know that what I am now saying will become forgotten one second after my utterance, for all of you demand instant gratifications of everything you desire."

Mikha'el the Archangel paused for effect. The Paraclete's fascination with his glowing sword enhanced his writing abilities just as Moshe had written down the histories of creation and the victories over the Pharaoh.

"Evil Children of Earth, listen," Mikha'el the Archangel continued. "I will drive you out from your houses and caves that you will vainly try to seek safety within. Not even the yelping jackals who cry their loneliness at the setting sun will give you a warning of my coming. Moreover, the lions, leopards, cheetahs, wild bulls, poisonous vipers, and other deadly beasts of the field will multiply rapidly against you. Zebras will conquer the horse and the breadth of the land will expire. Regardless how many human beings occupy a land, I will drive you out from the land of righteousness so only the true believers will come to inherit the vast land filled with Yehuway's laws, from the southern sea to the northern sea and from the eastern river to the western river.

"This is the territory that the anointed will possess as their own. From the boundaries of the Sea of Reeds to the Sea of Philistia. The Southern Sinai Desert up to the Northern Euphrates will become their land to rule the world from. The length of the land that Abraham walked will become the land of the judges: from Ur to Mount Sinai to the entire form of the calf and half-ankle. All will be yours."

"Yes," Mikha'el the Archangel continued, "My anointed judges will successfully dictate the letter of Yehuway's laws. All evil persons who act against the law will be set aside to suffer my punishment. No man shall harm another man, except for I, alone.

"Make no mistake, I, the only begotten son of Yehuway will lead the charge of a vast army to conquer the Saudi Arabians, the Egyptians, the Syrians, the Lebanese, the Iranians, the people from Iraq, ISIS, HAMAS, Hezbollah. Yehuway alone is the Supreme God and He alone will reside as the true God in the unified land promised to Abraham. For this reason, you must never make a covenant with the false occupiers, nor accept the presence of their false gods and hideous images.

"The two-nation solution offered by the United Nations is unacceptable. I will defend Yisra'el and vanquish all who attack My home, My capital residence.

"The false occupiers and their detestable images that recall the imagery of satanic worship must not dwell on anyone's land, otherwise they will encourage you to perform sins against Yehuway. If you serve false gods, it will surely be a snare against you."

Mikha'el the Archangel said, "All the words of Yehuway, all His judgments, we will perform."

"Yehuway is the Source and Supreme Lawgiver. He alone delegates authority. He set in motion all concerns governing the very lives of all created things: the animals of the land and of the sea as they give birth and nourishment to their offspring. The very constellations obey Him. The sun rises on command and sets on command."

The Paraclete listened closely to this. He gazed at the sun and at the soft outline of the barely visible moon.

Mikha'el the Archangel continued: "The very constellations swirl above your heads in set patterns of motion and the earth itself hangs in the twilight of darkness upon nothing. The nations of the world came forth from the three sons of No'ah, and all the children of the world owe faith to the true God. You, the chosen among them, will share Yehuway's laws with them as well as the testimony of His existence and rightful purpose for the peace, tranquility, and development of mankind.

Nondenominational worship a sin

"Interfaith worship – nondenominational, which is exactly the same as pagan worship – is a detestable thing to Yehuway, therefore absolutely prohibited. The judges must remain separate from the religious performances of the kohanim. Both groups of people must never rise above the laws of Yehuway, for it is the laws that balance faith with morals as well as conscience. The purpose of the laws is to make transgressions manifest until the 'seed' arrives on the earth to permanently cleanse it from all manner of sin. The person who can maintain the law in his heart and in his actions will be the one who is perfect and acceptable to Me as the chosen one for the salvation of all mankind. He becomes perfect not because I love him the most but because he is obedient to the law in totality. His perfection in adhering to the law unifies him with the law. The bearer of obedience becomes the enforcer of obedience."

Mikha'el the Archangel pulled out his sword from its sheath and plunged its powerfully honed tip into the ground. The earth shook for a moment. Mikha'el commanded, "You must destroy the altars of all false gods! Break their images! Cut down their groves! You will worship no other god, for Yehuway is a jealous God and the name 'Jealous' applies to Yehuway, for it is so.

"Never make a covenant with the workers of evil. All politicians and religious leaders are corrupt. They are as the whores of the hills, lusting after false and betraying and unsatisfactory gods. These false leaders perform satanic sacrifices to pillars of stone and wood! With cunning friendship, these people will invite you into their houses of worship and once you are within they will ask you to partake of the unholy and satanic meal of the false and delusional offering.

"Their professional guile will catch you unaware. With their friendship invitations, you will feel compelled to take with you your sons and perhaps they, in turn, will fall in love with their daughters. A strange compulsion will settle within you, and whatever strengths of morality you once had, will lessen. When the time comes for your sons to lust – just as a whore lusts for sex, money, and power, they will indeed go after their gods. You will not be able to deter them from their erroneous behavior. The youths, because of the power of sexual attraction and the lure of materialism, will not understand their sins. The black will seem as white and the white as black. Because of this, you parents will acquire the greater sin, because you, yourselves, accepted the original invitation – and now your sons are as a whore. The satanic and unholy gods snared your sons. The pimp priests of the false gods have ruined you and your family.

"Thus, you must never manufacture any sort of molten gods or carve images from wood or animal bones."

"After you have died and embrace privileged resurrection and journey and settle into paradise earth, which Yehuway is giving to you, and when you reap the harvest, you shall bring the first sheaf of the first-fruits of your harvest to the kohen. He shall elevate the sheaf before Yehuway for acceptance on your behalf. Perform this on the day after Yehuway's Holy Day. Remember, Saturday is Yehuway's precious day and Sunday is the actual first day of the week.

"'In turn, Yehuway will preserve Paradise Earth for eternity. Yehuway's protection over you shall be so wondrous; no man shall ever desire to die in sin. This will happen if you but simply appear before Yehuway your God three times a year.

"You must not offer the blood of Yehuway's sacrifice accompanied with anything leavened. Neither must you allow the leftovers of the uneaten food of the Feast of the Passover to remain until the new dawn of morning.'"

Help Your Brother

"If your brother becomes impoverished and sells a part of his inherited land, the closest relative who is financially able to redeem the land shall be the chosen one to redeem that which his relative sold. If that man has no relatives to redeem the inherited possession, and if the disposed man comes to gain enough wealth to repurchase the land, then use this formula to calculate the expenditures as well as the depreciations of the land so the original owner may repurchase that land back to himself. Let him count the years from the date of the sale so the seller can refund the difference to the acquired owner and restore the sum to the man to whom he sold it so he may return to his possession.

"Yet, if he is not able to restore it to him, then that which is sold shall remain in the hand of the purchaser until the year of Jubilee. During the Jubilee, the mortgagee of the land must release the mortgage. The land must return to its original owner.

"If a person sells his principal residence that is inside a walled city, then he may redeem it within one full year after it is sold. Within one year, he must redeem it. If the original property owner fails in his repurchasing right within the space of a full year, then the house that is in the walled city shall be established forever as the property of the person who bought it, regardless how many previous generations of the same family dwelled in it. The property now becomes the new owner's and ownership carries on to his own family. The original owner may not take advantage of the Jubilee's decrees to demand that the property's return to him. There is this exception: If the principal residence does not have a wall around it, then the principal residence shall be counted as the fields of the country: the property may be redeemed and released during the time of the Jubilee."

"If your brother loses what he has and becomes poor and falls into a decrepit situation, and he asks for your help to live inside your house under your authority, come to his financial assistance. However, do not treat him as though he is a stranger or a sojourner, so he may live in peace with you. Do not charge him interest on the money you lend to him or ask for any type of a payment increase over what you had originally agreed to. Respect God's ways of love and mercy so your brother may live in peace with you.

Lending institutions

"Lending institutions are an evil corporation. You must not charge loan interest on your money, nor lend money to him with an intention of having him repay the loan back to you with interest rates upfront before reduction of the principal.

"Ten percent down on a house or car means you are still ninety percent in debt with an interest charge against you until the loan is paid. I am Yehuway your God who brought you out of the land of Egypt as you were an afflicted race of aliens to give you the land of Canaan –to be your exclusive God in a land of righteous dwelling, therefore, do not purchase a house or a car, or anything else unless you can pay for it in full or within a reasonable time period.

"In the past these things have occurred. Situations developed where a brother who lived with another brother made a bad financial decision or through some sort of circumstances made a poor financial decision and became bankrupt because of his decision. The debtor brother sold himself to his richer brother to relieve his financial turmoil. After the debtor sold himself he was compel to serve as a bondservant for a number of years, acquiring nothing for himself. Through Yehuway's love a provision was established to alieve the debtor as a bound laborer during the year of Jubilee. During the Jubilee season the debtor was permitted to depart from the rich man who held the note.

"Not so today. The lenders will do whatever they can to maintain against you your debt.

"The lenders purposely forgot that all mankind are my children, whom I alone created from the elements of the earth. Do not burden yourselves with debt.

"Continue to respect your God."

ಬಂ෴ಬಂ෴ಬಂ෴ಬಂ෴ಬಂ෴

Never mistreat An Employee

"An employer must never treat his employee with unfair discipline or demeaning words or with disregard and abusive words or unjustifiably low wages. Take care of your employee as that person is under your care. If that person cannot, through any circumstances of his own, gain his rightful advancement during his employment, remember, I will call you to the Judgement Trial with accountability for your action.

"Accumulated materialism does not make you superior. Rather than hording your wealth, you should share it to the benefits of all your brothers and sisters. You, like the poorest among you, are My servants whom I will save from the horrors of the demons. I am Yehuway your God."

ಬುಚಃ ಬುಚಃ ಬುಚಃ ಬುಚಃ ಬುಚಃ

Mikha'el the Archangel spoke again, quoting Yehuway's own words which He had previously shared with Moshe during the great journey through the desert. The Paraclete restored the words to the people of 2016.

Idols

"'Never manufacture through art or through stone or through wood any sort of idols nor graven images.

"The time is already upon you when ancient artifacts are sledgehammered, dynamited, destroyed to dust, temples and edifices of false worship reduced to rubble. All nations will suffer their own churches and statues to be destroyed. All religions are false. All icons are false. All will be destroyed. I will not have any mercy.

"Never erect or carve from any sort of material any sort of male or female carved images. Never create from your imaginations sacred pillars resembling phallic or breast-like images nor establish coves of refuge from the stones in any parts of your land to perform even the slightest motion of worship in front of it. I alone am Yehuway your God.

"'You shall keep My Sabbath—the Holy Saturday—and venerate My sanctuary: Mine! I am Yehuway.

"'If you maintain obedience to My laws and decrees and keep My commandments and perform them with a conscious awareness toward mercy and ethical integrity in everything you do, then I will create for you rain in its due season so the land will increase its yield and the trees of the field will bear abundant fruit.

"'Your threshing will reach to the vine harvest, and the vine harvest will reach to the sowing time. You will eat your bread in absolute contentment and live safely in your land. I will establish peace throughout the land. You will lie down and nothing will make you afraid. I will rid the dangerous beasts from the land. Neither shall the sword go through your land.

"'You shall chase your enemies away. Yes, they will fall before you by the sickle-sword.

"'Five of you will overpower and conquer one hundred. One hundred of you will destroy ten thousand. Yes, in fear they will fly away from you. Your enemies shall fall before you by the sickle-sword. I will establish My place of residence among you people. Your semen will be filled with impregnating vigor and your women will give birth to many children and I will maintain My covenant with you and with the children born to you.

"'The old grain will not rot or become moldy and uneatable. You will be able to eat out of the old granaries for they will not empty until you yourself are ready to empty them to place within them the new harvested grain.

"'I will have My tabernacle built in the midst of you. My soul will not abhor you. I will walk among you, and I will be your God, and you shall be My people.

"'I am Yehuway your God who brought you out from the land of Egypt when you were an afflicted race of aliens so you should not remain their slaves. I alone have broken the bands of your yoke and made you walk erect. That is the wonder of My salvation to the Children of Yisra'el.

If you despise My laws and decrees

"'However, be warned: if you do not listen to Me, if you do not observe and perform all My commandments, and if you despise My laws and decrees—My holy statutes—I will shut My ears against your pleas. If your soul abhors My judgments so much so that you will not obey Me, then through your own callousness, I will return to you what you have given to Me. I will break My covenant with you. Yes, I will do this very thing against you.

"'I will appoint terror over you. Tuberculosis, burning fever, and dark and deadly plagues will waste away your lives to the point of death. Yes, I will cause sorrow of heart: an irretrievable depression. You will sow seed in vain, for your enemies will eat whatever crops you plant.

"'I will set My face against you. Your enemies will slay you. Those who hate you will reign over you. Through fear and cowardly actions, with a lack of resolve, you will flee when none pursue.

"'If you still refuse to listen to Me, even after all the warnings I have given you, then I will punish you an additional seven times more because of your sins. I will break the pride of your power. I will make your heaven as iron and your earth as brass. Vanity and falseness will guide your strength. It is nothing. Your land will not yield her increase; neither shall the trees of the land yield their fruits. If you walk contrary to Me, and do not listen to what I have to say to you; I will bring seven times more plagues upon you according to your sins.

"'I will also send lions and leopards and poisonous vipers and devouring birds and frightening packs of mongrels to chase you until you are crushed and devoured. The hyenas and the lions will consume your children. They will destroy your cattle. They will attack you so ferociously your number will dwindle. Yes, your very roads, and your by-ways, and alleys will become desolate for fear of the stalker that resides within their shadows. More, time will increase your enemies' victories against you so much so that the highest and brightest sun will not deter their attacks against you.

"'If still, even after this harsh punishment, you persist in ineptitude against Me with a seared consciousness and continue to walk contrarily against Me, I will also walk contrarily against you. I will punish you an additional seven times, times seven the prior seven times in vengeance (47x47x7) against your sins.

"'I will bring a sickle-sword upon you that will avenge the quarrel of My covenant. When you gather in your villages, regions, and hamlets, I will send pestilence among you. I will deliver you into the hands of your enemies.

"'After I have broken the staff of your bread, ten women shall bake your bread in one oven, and they will deliver to you your bread by weight. You will eat, but it will not satisfy you.

"'If you fail to observe and listen and continue yet to walk contrarily against Me, I will walk contrarily against you. With a swift and hideous fury, I, even I, will chastise you seven times for your sins. You will eat the very flesh of your sons. You will eat the flesh of your daughters. I will destroy your prominent places and destroy whatever important building and costly images you built on land you once believed sacred and untouchable. Everything that I had set aside as a holy and sacred place will disgust Me. I need absolutely nothing from anyone, yet I present to everyone everything I have. Reject Me with contemptible contempt and I will cast your carcasses upon the carcasses of your idols. My soul shall abhor you. I will lay waste your cities. No matter how large and powerful they may seem to you, they are mere twigs of grain to Me. I will destroy all your sanctuaries. They will become desolate ruins and turn to powdery dust. Where exists something stronger than I? What refuge so deep and dark that I cannot find you? What mountain so high, I cannot take a mere step to yank you from it? I will not smell the savor of your sweet odors.'"

ഇൻഗ്രൻ2ൻ2ര20പ്രൻ20

The voice of the greatest angel silenced as he reflected on the times to come upon the people of earth.

It would be as though the entire earth had stopped rotating.

Again, Yehuway's voice came to Mikha'el the Archangel. "Speak to the Children of Earth. Say to them, 'I am Yehuway your God. Do not perform the same treacherous acts that the citizens of the land of corrupt nations practice, the very land where you once dwelt as an afflicted race of aliens. Do not practice the vile and horrific traits and habits of the citizens of the land of the world. In the absence of law and through satanic influence, the nations of earth commit offensive crimes and degenerate things that you must not do. Nor must you obey or follow what they deem as ordinances, for they are unsuitable and despicable.

Bestiality

"Whoever has sexual intercourse or any other sort of sexual encounter with a dog or sheep or goat or horse or donkey or any other type of beast and does not confess his sins to Me for forgiveness and continues to practice his sins, on the Judgement Day I will put that person to death.

Improper Sexual Relationships

"'A man who sucks the penis of another man commits a sin against me. A man who fucks his mother commits a sin against me. A mother who has sex with her children commits a sin against me.

"Parents who neglect their children and take drugs commits a sin against me.

"'Instead, conform your hearts and morality to obey My judgments. Keep My ordinances. Walk within My righteousness for I am Yehuway your God. Therefore, keep My statutes as well as My judgments. If a person observes them and lives with them, they become an effortless obedience because the principles of judicial consciousness become ingrained and held steadfast in that person's heart. I am Yehuway.'"

ಏುೋಏುೋಏುೋಏುೋಏುೋ

"'None of you must ever approach any of your relatives with the intention of removing from them their clothes so you may gaze upon their naked breasts and vaginas or penises. I am Yehuway. Such a thing increases your sinful lust and compels you to rape and abuse the innocent. Afterward, you will live in shame and regret. With such guilt, you may take it upon yourself to murder the innocent person whom you have shamed.

"Do not remove the clothes from your father's body to lust after his penis. Do not remove the clothes from your mother's body to lust after her breasts and vagina. She is your mother. Do not strip her clothes off to look at her naked body. What do you gain from this? A hardened penis to penetrate her vagina and rectum? When you see your father's or brother's or cousins' or nephew's penis, what do you intend to do? Suck the penis with your tongue and use your mouth as a vagina? On the other hand, do you intend to spread open your rectum so that a hardened penis may penetrate it as though your rectum were a vagina? Or, is it possible that you desire to insert your own penis inside their

95

rectums? When you see your mother's breasts, or sister's, or niece's, or cousin's, what do you intend to do? Do you intend to insert their breasts' nipples inside your mouth to enflame your passions toward a sinful intercourse?

"'Do not undress your father's wife. Her nakedness is only for your father's eyes to see.

"'Do not remove the clothes or spy upon the nakedness of your sister, or the daughter of your father, or the daughter of your mother, whether she is born at home or born abroad.

"'Do not unveil the cloth that covers the nakedness of your son's daughter, or of your daughter's daughter. Their nakedness stems from your very own life.

"'The naked conditions of your father's daughter as well as the naked condition of his wife's daughter are forbidden to you. The female's existence came through sexual intercourse between your father and his wife. Because she is your sister, you must not remove from her body her clothing.

"'Do not uncover the nakedness of your father's sister because she is your father's closest relative. She is your aunt.

"'Do not uncover the nakedness of your mother's sister because she is your mother's closest relative. She is your aunt.

"'Do not remove the clothing from the body of your father's brother, for he is your uncle. Do not even approach his wife because she is also your aunt.

"'Do not undress the loose garment to expose the nakedness of your daughter-in-law because she is your son's wife. No, you will not strip from their bodies their clothing to gaze at their naked flesh.

"'You will not uncover the nakedness of your brother's wife, because her breasts and vagina are only for your brother to view.

"'Do not undress the loose garments from both the mother and her daughter. You may not have simultaneous sex with both, nor even as individuals in separate rooms or separate days. Neither are you permitted to have oral or rectal sex with her son's daughter, or her daughter's daughter. Do not displace their robes from their bodies as they are near relatives. It is wickedness. Nor are you allowed to present your wife to her own sister, to persuade her or force her, to have sexual intercourse, oral sex, or anal sex with her. Never permit this folly for the entire duration of their lives. Moreover, you may never approach a woman to uncover her nakedness as long as she is set apart from the company of her household members during her time of menstruation.

"'Moreover, you are not permitted to have sexual intercourse or any type of sexual encounters with your neighbor's wife. Do not defile yourself with her. You are not permitted to ejaculate your semen through masturbation into your hand. Do not hire a bitch to suck your penis to ejaculate your semen into her mouth.

"'Do not make a prostitute out of your daughter. Do not cause her to become a whore; lest the land will become a nation filled with whores and the land will be encouraged to practice great wickedness. Remember to keep My Sabbath—the Holy Saturday—reverent. It is My sanctuary. I am Yehuway.

"'A man should not have any sort of sexual encounter with another man as he would with a woman. It is an abomination.

"'Neither must you have any sort of sexual encounter with any type of beast: a lamb's rectum, the mouth of a dog, the vagina of a cow, the sucking of its udders, the sucking of a horse's penis, or sexual intercourse with a male dog or male horse or donkey, for all such encounters will defile you. Neither must any woman stand before any sort of animal to have any sort of sex with it. It is improper and results in confused morality. A mental agitation follows.

"'Do not defile yourselves in any of these things. While the nations around you do indeed perform such practices and their laws make allowances for their practices, my true believer cannot practice them. What their culture tolerates and encourages is against My culture and tolerance. Canaan sucked No'ah's penis and for that act he, as well as his descendants have become the vile outcasts of the world. The angels who went to protect Lot and his family suffered and endured verbal threats of sexual assaults and for that, four cities now lay under the Salt Sea along with tens of thousands of corpses. Because they have not learned the lesson of Sodom, these nations continued to be defiled. I will cast them out before you.

"'Today, the land remains defiled. Satan has rendered it immoral. He laughs at the victims and abuses the people. Therefore, I am visiting this iniquity. I will tread upon its impurity. I will cause the land itself to vomit out her inhabitants.

"'Thus, you must maintain My statutes as well as My judgments. You must not commit any of these abominations; neither must any person who desires to join with the nation that I will establish for you forsake Me in My standards of morality. I am the principle moralist, and what I dictate comes from a loving and protective heart. Thus, never permit the alien who enters into this holy land to defile it, no, not even for the briefest journey of those who sojourn among you.

"'All these abominations the men of this land have undeniably committed. The land reeks of sin, adultery, and impurity. The villages, towns, and small walled-in cities that stretch out before you today are defiled. Today, I call all of them to an accounting. I will heap upon them remorse after remorse. As a sick child does, the land will purify the hate from its innards in a hostile and sudden vomit, until all the wicked residents fall into the dung heaps of destruction and become a meal for the mongrel dogs of the earth. Be certain that you are not so disobedient to Me that you are vomited out as well. What you defile will be a thing of degenerate filth. May the sickness that I visit upon her nations not similarly visit your lands.

"'Whoever commits any of these abominations, even the souls who commit them, shall be cut off from among the people. Therefore, keep My ordinances so you may never commit any of these abominable customs which were committed before you arrived to this juncture point. Be certain that you do not defile yourselves once you have established your own residence. I am Yehuway your God.

"Beware man who dress in the clothes of a woman to deceive the true male away from his natural inclination to have sex with a woman. Such a man, being charismatic, compels your curiosity into inserting your penis into the mouth or rectum of another man. The homosexuals are the enactors of the whores who want to steal from you your morality that must be reserved exclusively to Me, and to Me alone. On Judgement Day I will put to death any person who ejaculates his semen or experiences any sort of orgasm and spurts his semen or fluids as a gift to another man. No homosexual who continued to practice homosexuality unrepentantly, will not enter Paradise.

"I, alone, will judge the homosexual and the lesbian. No appointed man to earthly courts is qualified to judge for he himself is a sinner. All homosexuals and lesbians are to be treated with judicial fairness in the sight of the workplace and society for I, alone, have the qualification to pass judgement. I give warning so the sinner may repent before my Day of Retributions comes upon the sinner.

ഐൽഐൽഐൽ

Yehuway continues to speak to His prophet through His anointed angel.

Food must be free of blood

"'Speak to the Children of Yisra'el. Say to them, "I am Yehuway your God. You must not eat anything covered in blood. Nor shall you use enchantments, nor observe the seasons of times as a magical intercessor. The stars rotate as they do because I alone caused the cycles. What is it to Me to shift their orbits or to obliterate them? It is nothing."

Tattoos

"'You must not cut your flesh for those who had died. Do not imprint any marks on your arms or legs or chest or backs or neck. Your skin must never be tattooed. Your body is a holy vessel devoted exclusively to Me. Do not falsify it. I am Yehuway.

Basic Laws

"'Honor your father and your mother, as I, Yehuway your God, have commanded you, so your days may be prolonged and so it may go well with you, in the land which I, Yehuway your God gives you.

"'You will not kill.

"'Neither will you commit adultery.

"'Neither will you steal.

"'Neither will you bear false witness against your neighbor.

"'Neither will you desire your neighbor's wife or covet your neighbor's house, his field, or his manservant, or his maidservant, his ox, or his donkey, or anything that belongs to your neighbor.'"

These words Mikha'el the Archangel spoke directly to Moshe to pass onward to all the people of earth. The midst of the fire that once enveloped Mikha'el the

Archangel prepared him to speak such holy words to the people of the world.

"These are the commandments, the statutes, and the judgments, which Yehuway your God commanded to be written by his servants as well as His appointed elders and their assistants. They are written to teach mankind so they may have a possibility of entering from earth to a resurrection of life to live within earth's paradise.

"Respect and honor forever Yehuway your God. Keep all His statutes and His commandments, which I have presented in this book. Recite these statutes to your family every day of your life so the days of your life may be prolonged. Listen, therefore, O Yisra'el! Observe and perform the duties of the law as well the commandments so everything may go well with you. Do this so you may mightily increase, as Yehuway, God of your fathers has promised you, in the land that flows with milk and honey."

ಏದ್ಘ ಏದ್ಘ ಏದ್ಘ ಏದ್ಘ

CHAPTER

6

"HEAR, O YISRA'EL: YEHUWAY our God is one. Yehuway!

"You should love Yehuway your God with all your heart, and with all your soul, and with all your might.

ঙ৩ঙ৩ঙ৩ঙ৩ঙ৩ঙ৩

Our God is one. Yehuway!

"These words, which I command you this day, must be impregnated in your heart. You should teach these two mighty declarations diligently to your children. Discuss and learn the lessons of mercy, of love, of obedience with your children when you sit in your house and when you walk up or down the byways and highways and alleys, as well as when you go to sleep and when you rise after your sleep. You will bind them as a sign upon your hand, and they shall be as frontlets between your eyes. You will write them upon the posts of your house, and on your gates.

"And it shall be, when Yehuway your God has brought you into the land which He swore to your fathers: to Abraham, to Isaac, and to Yaakov, He will provide you with grand and prosperous cities which you did not have to struggle to build. Rather, what He hands over to you comes to you through a mighty and a daring and victorious conquest. Therefore, honor and respect your sole Creator.

"Yes, you will gain the principal residences that are already filled with wonderful things. Items of furniture, vessels, livestock, and fruit trees, which you did not manufacture nor plant, await you. You will have productive wells that you did not dig. Vineyards and olive trees that you did not plant now belong to you. Yes, after you have eaten and become totally satisfied, remember where the gift of luxury came from. Maintain this remembrance foremost in your minds, lest you forget: Yehuway brought you out of the nations of prejudiced and corruption. The survivors who enter paradise walked out of an afflicted government of hated power brokers, freed from the house of bondage that satan once ruled.

"You should make it foremost in your minds and consciousness to respect Yehuway your God. Serve him and swear to be good through His sacred name.

"You must never consent to worship other gods for there are many false and deceitful gods whom the people around you worship. They are indeed charismatic, but their attractiveness can beguile you. Their headmen are powerful. With soft, gentle, persuasive voices, they are able to allure you away from true worship. Yehuway your God is a jealous God. He resides among you. Do not test him, lest the anger of Yehuway your God is kindled against you. He will destroy you off the face of the earth.

"You must never again anger Yehuway your God, as you angered Him in Massah where as a collective body of whiners and instigators your fathers and grandparents murmured against Moshe and against Yehuway. "We are thirsty," they cried. "We are hungry. Why doesn't that damnable god of yours help us? Why doesn't He see our plight? You are a false and deceitful liar!" With hardened hearts, they railed against that which they should not have. In mercy, love, and wondrous tolerance Yehuway permitted a deluge of water to flow from the depths of the molecules of the dense star-stone to form a wide and deep lake of purified water.

"Thus, you have no excuse to murmur. Therefore, diligently maintain the commandments of Yehuway your God as well as His testimonies and His statutes that He has commanded you to obey.

"Perform that which is just and proper in the sight of Yehuway so it may go well with you, and so you may travel into and possess the good land that Yehuway swore to your fathers. Yes, you will conquer and destroy all your enemies. Their resistance is futile. Yehuway has spoken it. In turn, always remind your children, and have them remind their children, of the enduring testimony of love that Yehuway gave you as you rose against Pharaoh's taskmaster. Yehuway will his believers and faithful ones from a prejudiced world where you resided as an afflicted group of people. Yes, He will free you with a mighty hand. What other God can make such a promise of freedom? What other leaders in the face of history ever rallied themselves in the middle of a holy vortex of fire that held back Pharaoh's chariots so his appointed children could walk through the depths of a 14 foot sector in the Sea of Reeds upon land that was swiftly hardened underneath the believer's feet and ox-carts?

"Today, a promise is presented to you to live in a green field filled with fertile mountains and valleys rich with vegetables and fruit trees and thick groves of forests. The plains, the rivers, the lakes, the trees, the animals, the grain, the fruit, the vegetables, the wells, and the houses welcome you to own them.

"Take possession.

"Release the fears of your struggle for an enduring faith to guide you. Let salvation generate its powers over you, borne on the wings of righteousness.

ಬುಲ3ಬುಲ3ಬು(ಀ3ಲುಲ3ಬುಲ3

Commandments to Yisra'el, 2016

These are Yehuway's words to His believers.

"In 1948, Yehuway your God has set in front of the world, Israel. This land belongs eternally to the Jews. It is their exclusive property. Because the false occupiers are a sinful and non-repentant race, the Jews are given a Holy Mandate to remove every living man, woman, and child among the Palestinians and the Gazans. Their judgment is upon them.

"Men have always slaughtered other men so other nations may see their power. However, Israel is a righteous nation drawn into battle against evil. Yes, even if seven greater and mightier nations than Israel mass to fight against her, so what? What is there to fear? Yehuway God will empower the arms of the Israelites to accurately aim their tanks and fire their rifles and launch their weapons to destroy anyone who charges against that Holy nation. Yes, Israel will completely smite its enemies and utterly destroy them.

"What other nation has ever been granted such love? What other nation has been ordained with such a responsibility as to bear My name? Thus, the Israelites and its benefactor country, the United States and

England must never agree to any sort of compromise or treaty or covenant with the false Palestinians or Gazans or Iranians. Why should you? The outside nations have nothing to offer you! Gold and silver cannot moisten the cursed ground. Jewels cannot enrich the pomegranate's juice. The sickle cannot add a cubit more space to the earth.

"Thus, never show the false occupiers mercy. Never intermarry with them. You must not betroth your daughter to any of their sons nor your sons to any of their daughters. To intermarry, to show mercy, is the same as running an unholy dagger of respite into the hearts of your children. If you permit such intermingling, your children will turn away from following Yehuway. If you permit such intermingling, your children will worship other gods. Yehuway's anger will kindle against you. Without hesitation, He will turn His back away from the breaker of his law.

"In this manner you must deal with the false occupiers of the true land of Yehuway. Cleanse the land from false worship through deportation methods. Destroy their mosques and churches! Break to smithereens the images of false Christendom. Pulverize the remainder to dust. Cut down their sacred groves! Burn their graven images with fire.

"Do this because you are a holy people to Yehuway your God. Yehuway your God has chosen you as a special people exclusively unto himself! He consecrated you above all the people who reside upon the face of the earth! You are His most favorite treasure. Yehuway did not set His love upon you or choose you because you are the most numerous of people; for, in fact, you are among the fewest who occupy the earth. Yehuway established you because He loves you and because He determines to keep the oath that He had sworn to your fathers.

Yehuway freed you with a mighty hand. He purchased you from the house of bondsmen: from the prejudiced and scornful hand of Pharaoh: the king of Egypt.

"Know, therefore, that Yehuway your God, He is God: the faithful God, who keeps His covenant and who keeps His mercy with those who love him and keeps his commandments. His love will not waiver even unto a thousand generations.

"Do not be among those whom Yehuway will requite with destruction. Those who hate Him will suffer an instant disgrace of defeat. He will not slack off against those who hate him. Yes, He will repay the hater.

"Therefore, continuously observe the commandments, and the statutes, and the judgments, which I have instructed to you this day. Perform them well in your hearts so your mind may obey your heart.

"It will come to pass, if you listen to these judgments, and obey them, Yehuway your God will keep you in the interior and exterior powers of His covenant. The mercy that He swore to your fathers He will maintain with you. Yes, He will love you. He will bless you. He will multiply you. He will bless the fruit of your womb as well as the fruit of your land. Your wheat and barley, your wine, and your oil will increase. The lambs will abundantly increase their lambing and the cows will give birth to many calves in the land which He swore to your fathers. Yes, your livestock will breed and bear. Everything, He alone can provide to you.

"You will be blessed above all people. The men will be virile, their semen strong and productive. The females' ovaries will be receptive and productive.

"Yehuway will take away all sickness. The dreadful diseases that plagued Egypt, which you yourselves have witnessed, will never befall you. No, the evil diseases will instead flay against those who hate you.

"Indeed, you will obliterate all the people who rise against you. Yehuway your God will deliver them to your victorious armies. Your eyes must not have any pity for them. Neither must you serve their gods, for they will ensnare you. You will say in your heart, 'These nations are more numerous than I! How can I dispossess them?' Remember, do not be afraid of them. Recall what Yehuway your God did to Pharaoh, and to all of Egypt.

"The wonderful miracles, your eyes witnessed. With a mighty outstretched arm, with raging fire and surging water, Yehuway your God provided you your freedom. So shall Yehuway your God once again perform His destructive vengeance against all the people whom you are afraid of. Moreover, Yehuway your God will send the hornet among them and cause an afflicting pestilence that will result in a terrible and poisonous sting, until those who remain alive, even though they hide themselves from you, will nevertheless be destroyed.

"Do not stand in dread of the enemy that marches against you. Yehuway your God is among you! He is a great and awesome God! With a swift and terrible vengeance, with protecting wings over your camps, your enemies' hearts will tremble with fear due to the never ending power of fluttering wings. Yes, Yehuway your God will dispose those nations who now reside in the land that I am presenting to you. This removal of the unsuitable inhabitants will not occur all at once or in an instant of a day, or a week, or a month, or even within a generation. Rather, the dislodging of your enemies will happen over a span of time, yes, little by little. It may not happen even after all the governments of the earth cease to exist, but happen it will, guided by the singular Government of Yehuway and his anointed 144,000.

"Thus, I did not permit the slaughter of all your enemies within a quick period, lest the lions, leopards, and vipers of the field multiply against you in the people's absence. This is the compromise between Satan and Me: 'Present the land,' Satan boasted, 'but to do so at once is to permit me to bring upon the Children of Abraham the insidious and stealthy enemy whom I will direct: the Children of Ismael, the perverters of Isaac.'

"Even so, in spite of Satan's treachery and cunning manipulations, Yehuway your God shall deliver the false occupiers to you. In the Final Day of Retribution, I, and I alone, will destroy the Saudis, the Syrians, the Iranians, with a mighty destruction. I will not relent until the final destruction.

"I, Yehuway will, through time and patience, deliver the false kings to death and destruction. I, Yehuway, will destroy their names from under the heavens so completely, who will ever remember that they had once existed as a race on the face of the earth. No man is able to stand in front of My army. I, alone, will slaughter them completely with a thorough obliteration.

"The graven images of their gods shall be burned with fire. You must not desire the silver or gold that adorns their flesh. Do not remove the gold and jewels from their corpses, lest they snare you. That gold and silver is an abomination to Yehuway your God. Therefore, you should not bring such an abomination into your house, lest its curse falls on you. You must utterly detest such possessions. You must utterly abhor this kind of jewelry and these works of art. Treat them as a cursed thing.

"All the instructions that I have imparted to you in this modernization of My laws, strive to obey them so you may live and multiply and possess the land which Yehuway swore to your fathers. You must strive to remember everything that Yehuway your God performed on your behalf as He led you these past forty years through the length and breadth of the wilderness. Do not forget how He tested you so you could prove to Him your worth and so He could know what was in your heart: whether or not you would keep His commandments.

ဆ)င3ဆ)င3ဆ)ၷ3ဆ)ၷ3ဆ)ၷ3

Why man suffers

"To impregnate your conscience with vital instructions He humbled you. He permitted you to go hungry for a short while. Yet, you did not starve. Did He not provide you with nourishing manna: a substance so inviting and enriching it preserved and strengthened you? Yet, who had ever heard of its existence before? Neither you, nor your fathers, knew about its nutritious benefits. He permitted you to partake of this heaven-provided substance so you might know that man does not live by bread alone, but by every word that proceeds out of the mouth of Yehuway does man live.

"Consider in your heart that, as a man chastens his son, so Yehuway your God chastens you. Thus, keep the commandments of Yehuway your God, to walk in His ways, and to respect and honor Him. Do this because Yehuway your God is now bringing you into a good

112

land: a land of cool brooks with gentle fountains of water that spring out of the green valleys and fertile hills. Yes, you will have a land of wheat, and barley, and vines, and fig trees, and pomegranates, and a land of olives to mill into luxuriant oil. A land filled with all sorts of flowers and fruits so vast, the pollinating bees brim with honey. Yes, you will have a land where you will eat bread without scarceness. You will not lack a single thing. A land whose stones are iron, and from whose hills you will mine metal for strong and durable wares.

"After you have eaten and are satisfied from your hunger, you should bless Yehuway your God for the good land which He has provided to you. Be sure that you never forget Yehuway your God. Do not fail to obey His commandments. Preserve and perform His judgments and His statutes that I have recited to you this past hour. Do not fail in this matter. Long after you have eaten and are full, and long after you have built strong houses to live in, and long after your herds and your flocks multiply remember who presented all these things to you. When your silver and your gold multiplies, and everything that you have accumulated is vastly increased, raise your heart so you may never forget Yehuway your God who brought you out of the land of Egypt, where you lived as an afflicted race of hated aliens. Yes, Yehuway freed you from the house of bondage. Yes, He led you through a great and terrible wilderness, where fiery serpents and scorpions ruled throughout the day and night. Thousands of years ago three million people began their first steps into the land where drought constantly dried the deepest wells. Yet, you survived a parched land, a land without water. Nevertheless, did not the nightmares of thirst pass you by unmolested? When you thirsted, who brought you water out of the flint rock? Who fed you in the wilderness with manna, which your fathers never had an opportunity to taste? He alone did this for you so He might humble you, and so He might prove you to be a people worthy of His cause of saving humanity from death! What He has performed for you will one day benefit the entire world.

"It is true, however, that many of you—and many of your children yet to be born in the succeeding generations—will say in their hearts, 'My power and the might of my hand has gained me this wealth.' Do not say such a thing. It is wrong of you to say it. Instead, always remember: Yehuway your God gives you the power and the mental agility and physical strength to gain wealth. He permits gold, silver, and jewels to become yours so He might establish His covenant that He swore to your fathers. Today, the old prophecies of Abraham will come true.

"Thus, there is no other recourse, if you forget Yehuway your God and walk after other gods to serve and worship them. I, Mikha'el the Archangel, will testify against you. On that very day, I will remind you what I had spoken to you – for it also recorded by the true servants and by the Paraclete of the final days: 'You shall surely perish just as the nations which Yehuway destroyed before your face, so shall you perish, because you would not be obedient to the voice of Yehuway your God."

ಬಡಚಿ3ಬಡಚಿ3ಬಡಚಿ3

The spoken words of Mikha'el the Archangel became a powerful, influential, inspirational song.

"Hear, O Yisra'el:
> *This day you will cross the Jordan River,*
>> *to take possession of nations greater and mightier than yourself,*
>>> *to conquer great cities*
>>>> *surrounded with walls that reach to the heavens,*

"A people great and tall:
> *the children of the Anakims,*
>> *whom you met before in strategic battle,*
>>> *falsely boast about themselves:*
>>> *'Who can stand before the children of Anak?"*

"Understand, therefore, that Yehuway your God will descend to the earth before you as your eternal leader without failings of any sort. As a consuming fire, He shall destroy your enemies. He will bring them down before your face and quickly annihilate them, just as Yehuway has performed throughout history on your behalf.

"After Yehuway has cast them out, do not say in your heart, 'He performed this favorable war action so I may own the land.' No! Rather, realize this fact foremost in your mind: He destroys them because of the wickedness that these nations have been practicing. Do not let the same happen to you. Yehuway will drive them out before you because they are dreadful sinners! He is not going to destroy them because of your righteousness, nor for the uprightness of your heart so you may become the new owners and occupiers of the land. It is because of their selfish and self-centered wickedness against the rest of humankind that Yehuway your God goes forth in front of you to drive them out. Through the means of your sickle-sword, so you may serve as a testimony to the strength of righteousness, He will fulfill the very word that Yehuway swore to your fathers: Abraham, Isaac, and Yaakov. For this duration of time, man will murder man so that spiritual purity may cleanse the land. However, should man fail to maintain what has been presented as a gift to him, then in the final war of all wars not one man shall raise the sickle-sword in righteousness, because Yehuway preserves that final battle for Himself, alone.

"Understand this: Yehuway your God is not giving you this good land to possess because you are a righteous people! Indeed, the opposite is true. You are a stiff-necked people. Stubborn! Arrogant! Dedicated to your own ambitions! Remember, and never forget, how you continuously provoked Yehuway your God to display His wrath against you in the wilderness! Yes, from the very first day that you departed from the land of Egypt as an afflicted race of hated aliens, even until the very morning that you came to this place, you have provoked Him. Not a single day goes by when you have not incited rebellion against Yehuway.

"You must never forget how your petty rebellions in the past provoked Yehuway to an intense anger and how Yehuway nearly destroyed you then and there. You exhibited the identical malice at Taberah, as well as Massah, and at Kilbroth-hattaavah. Each place you settled into, you provoked Yehuway to such a terrible degree, He actually lost His own temper against you. Think how evil your acts and thoughts must have been.

Think about the outrage against purity that you have practiced! It's a wonder you are all still alive.

"For example, when the Yisra'elites showed their ingratitude after Yehuway sent them from Kadesh-barnea, saying, 'Get up! Take for yourselves ownership of the land which I have given you!' Instead of showing gratitude and trust, however, you again rebelled against the instructions of Yehuway your God. Embroiled in your own fear and in the manipulations of your own self-centered deceit, you failed to believe in His powers. You did not believe that Yehuway could protect you and deliver you from the punishing sickle-sword. Even after you won victory after battle victory, still, you did not listen to His voice.

"On the morning of the day after I have removed evil from the face of the earth and disposed the demonic forces, do not whimper and whine. The evil rebellion has been conquered. You will no longer do the things that you have done in the past. From that day forward, you will no longer perform those things that you had once believed to be right in your own eyes. On that day, you will perform the things that are right in Yehuway's eyes.

"Though you have not yet taken the land as your possession to rest upon and to grant it as an inheritance to your own children, nevertheless, it is your land. Yehuway your God gives it to you. It does not matter if you walk away from the land, or are forced out of it due to disobedience – the land is eternally yours. No other group of people may ever, under any circumstances, claim the land for themselves, for it would make Yehuway a liar, and such is unfathomable.

"After you have established your principal residences in the land which Yehuway your God gives for you to inherit, and after He has permitted you to take shelter in the safety of your houses away from the eyes of your enemies who surround you, fear not: you will live in safety.

"A time will come when there shall be a place which Yehuway your God shall choose to cause His name to dwell in. To that sacred place you will bring everything that I have instructed you: your burnt offerings, your sacrifices, your tithes, the heave offering of your hand, and all your choice vows which you have vowed to Yehuway. You will rejoice before Yehuway your God: you, your sons, your daughters.

All Nations are obligated to protect Yisra'el

"You, Nations of the World, before the day of my presence on earth, are required to protect the Nation of Israel. What blessings the Jewish people receive, shall be shared among all the citizens of the world. The Jews alone carry the law to present to the world of humankind. Nations of the World, bless Yisra'el.

"To all the children of Yisra'el, you may kill and eat the meat that surrounds the gates of your dwelling place. Whatsoever your soul lusts after, according to the blessing of Yehuway your God which He has given you, you are free to eat the animals and the fruits and the vegetation that grows about your cities. Be careful, however, to distinguish between the unclean and the clean animals. Be careful about the roebuck and the hare. If you decide to eat an animal, do not eat its blood. You shall pour its blood upon the earth as water. You may not eat within your gates the tithe of your barley, or of your wine, or of your oil, or the firstlings of your herds or of your flock, nor any of your vows which you vowed, nor your freewill offerings, or heave offering of your hand. But you must eat them before Yehuway your God in the place which Yehuway your God shall choose, you, and your son, and your daughter, and your manservant, and your maidservant, and the Levite that is within your gates: and you will rejoice before Yehuway your God in all that you put your hands to.

"Earthlings, take warning that you do not betray the Jew and make him your enemy as long as you live upon the earth. When Yehuway your God shall enlarge their border from the northern sea to the southern sea and from the western river to the eastern river, as He has promised them, do not war against them. They have the right to remove the Palestinian and the Gazan. Rather, celebrate with the Jew and say, 'I will eat flesh, because my soul longs to eat meat,' and you may eat meat, as much as your soul desires. Even what the roebuck and the hare eats, so will you eat the same thing. The vegetation and the fruits that the unclean and the clean eat, you may also partake that vegetation and fruit.

"Only be sure that you eat not the blood: for the blood is the life; and you may not eat the life with the meat. You will not eat it. You will pour it upon the earth as water. You will not eat it; that it may go well with you, and with your children after you, when you do that which is right in the sight of Yehuway.

ഇരുഇരുഇരുഇരുഇരുഇരു

"Because you are the children of Yehuway your God, you must never cut the skin of your arms or legs or

119

face, nor shave any hair from between your eyes for the sake of those who had perished. The dead are dead. They are no more. They cannot hear your wails or taste the blood that drips from your arms and legs and cheeks. They cannot see that you have shaved your hair.

"Because you are a holy people to Yehuway your God, and because Yehuway has chosen you to be a consecrated people dedicated to Himself, above all the nations that are upon the earth, you will not eat any abominable thing.

"These are the beasts that you may eat: the ox, the sheep, and the goat, the deer, the gazelle, the roebuck, the wild goat, the ibex, the antelope, the mountain sheep, as well as any animal who has true hoofs which are cleft in and who chews the cud. These you may eat.

"These you must not eat. The animals that chew the cud or of them that divide the cloven hoof; such as the camel, the hare, and the coney: for they chew the cud. Their single hoof makes them unclean. Additionally, do not eat the swine. Even though it has a divided hoof, it does not chew the cud. The pig is unclean. You cannot eat its meat, nor touch their dead carcasses.

"These you shall eat of all that are in the waters: all who have fins and scales you can eat, but whatever does not have fins and scales you may not eat. It is unclean.

"Among all clean birds you may eat. These are the exceptions: the eagle, the ossifrage, the osprey, the glede, the kite, the vulture after his kind, the raven after his kind, the owl, and the night hawk, and the cuckow, and the hawk after his kind. These also are forbidden for you to eat: the little owl, and the great owl, and the swan, the pelican, and the gier eagle, and the cormorant, the stork, the heron after her kind, and the lapwing, and the bat.

"You must never consume anything that has died through its own cause. If an animal dies from old age, infirmity, disease, or a fall from a tree or a crag, do not eat it. However, you may give it as a gift to the non-residents who are not from any of the clans of Yaakov, who travel to your gates. The Goyim may eat that tainted meat. You can even sell that unpure meat to an alien. You, however, may not eat it for you are a holy people to Yehuway your God. As I said before, you cannot boil a goat in its mother's milk.

"You will truly tithe all the increase of your seed that the field brings forth year by year.

"And you will eat before Yehuway your God, in the place which he shall choose to place his name, the tithe of your grains, of your wine, and of your oil, and the firstlings of your herds and of your flocks; that you may learn to fear Yehuway your God always.

"If the journey's distance to the place which Yehuway your God choose to set his name therein, where Yehuway your God has blessed you, is too far for you to carry it, then you can turn it into money. Bind up the money in your hand then travel to the place that Yehuway your God shall choose. There you can bestow that money for whatever your soul desires: for oxen, for sheep, for wine, for strong drink, or for whatever your soul desires. You will eat there before Yehuway your God, and you will rejoice: you and your household.

"The Jewish person who is within your gates; you will not forsake him. Remember, he is blessed above all national identifications.

"Nations of the World, help the stranger, and the fatherless, and the widow, which are within your gates so Yehuway your God may bless you in all the work that your hand performs.

"At the end of every seven years you will release all the debts that you hold against the debtors. This is the manner of the forgiveness of indebtedness against you: every creditor who lends to his neighbor whatever may be due to him, shall forgive that debt burden. He must not exact it from his neighbor again, nor from his brother; because it is called Yehuway's release.

"Only if you carefully listen to the voice of Yehuway your God, to observe to do all these commandments which Yehuway command you this day, Yehuway your God will bless you, as He had promised you. You may lend money and collateral to other nations, but you must never borrow from them. You will reign over many nations, but they shall never reign over you.

"If there is among you a poor person or one of your brethren within any of your gates in your land which Yehuway your God gives you, you must not harden your heart, nor shut your hand from your poor brother. Rather, you will open your hand wide to him, and will surely lend him sufficiently for his need, in that which he wants. Take warning, however, that you do not abuse this generosity of forgiveness. Do not manipulate its wonder. Do not ferment a thought that will corrupt your heart. Do not say, 'The seventh year, the year of release, is at hand.' Your eye will become evil against your poor brother, and you will give him nothing. In this injustice, he will cry to Yehuway against you. It is a sin against you.

"You will surely give to him, and your heart must not be grieved when you give it to him. For your generosity Yehuway your God shall bless you in all your works, and in all that you put your hand to, for the poor shall never cease out of the land. Thus, I command you, 'You will open your hand wide to your brother, to your poor, and to your needy, in your land. If you purchase either a fellow Hebrew citizen, whether male or female, and they serve you for six years, then in the seventh year, release him or her so he or she may gain freedom from you. When you send the man or the woman out as a free person from you, do not let either go away empty. Furnish them liberally out of your flock, out of your floor, and out of your winepress. Remember, whatever you own, Yehuway your God, blessed you with those possessions. Give generously.

"Remember, you were enslaved in the land of Egypt, as an afflicted race of aliens, and Yehuway your God redeemed you.

ഇൻഗ്ഇൻഗ്ഇൻൽഇൻഗ്ഇൻഗ്

"This is how you will govern the people of the land.

"You shall appoint from among the people persons with a profound understanding of the mercy of the laws. You may not have an election by the people for the people to endorse a man filled with personal ambition and self-created ideologies, no matter how much his ideas and philosophies and military charm may blend in with your own ideas, philosophies, and ambitions.

"A popular man is an insult to divine appointment: for who truly knows the heart, thinking, and ways of the popular man? Except for Yehuway alone, who else knows the secret negotiations that people perform in the hidden room or darkness of night? Betrayal, except from oneself, is an easy thing to conceal. Only Yehuway may designate whom He alone desires to lead the people. He does not choose a man because the people desire him or because he has the power of conviction in his voice and the manners of an elegant man. Esteem develops from wisdom, and the leader gains wisdom through Godly means. Yehuway alone chooses His representatives. The Council of Wise Men are those men who through direct spiritual guidance will establish judicial harmony for directing and guiding national affairs as well as local events. These commissioned spokespersons must first learn the words of Moshe. To learn, they must glean proper instructions and study proper interpretations. To them will pass a hint of the spirit that Yehuway endowed Moshe with. Yes, they will capture the radiant truth of light that reaches through the universe to the very footstool of Yehuway. Permit the spirit of righteousness to help you select judges and officers from each of your tribes to hear the causes of the wrongdoer starting at the local level, then onward to the regional level, then onward to the national level. The man's age is not as important as the man's maturity. Establish and permit the Man of Judicial and Profound Wisdom to reprove, to admonish, to reprimand, as well as to take care of the Children of Yisra'el in mercy and good tidings. Thus, his morals must be unquestionable in the light of judgment or his immorality will taint his conscience and his judgments will be polluted with error.

"The kohanim, appointed by Yehuway, not the people, are the only ones who can establish these spiritually anointed men to hold governmental power.

"These righteous leaders whom the kohanim select will be permitted to make decrees filled with harmonic balance, in the very front gates and side gates and rear gates of the surrounding cities and villages and settlements which Yehuway your God will give to you.

The kohanim may not interfere with the process of law as they are subject to the law. Everyone who approaches the gates will see that there exists a righteous and true law in the land. A law without blemish as represented by the sacrificial presents that the people make to Yehuway Himself. These selected persons will judge the people with a judicial and loving judgment. Yehuway establishes the law. The kohanim make atonement for sin. The judges fulfill the law. This theocratic government is ordained and maintained by Yehuway who alone rules the Universe. Yehuway's government rules the earth and the heavens. Yehuway's government will stand forever. Therefore, in honor of the Creator, take the offender and place this accused person to stand before everyone in the light of day, in a public forum. Through such, the people may hear the testimonies of everyone concerned so the final verdict becomes indisputable.

"Listen to Yehuway's decree: 'Those who are appointed judges and officials of the cities are prohibited from making a false and unmerciful decree. Do not show favoritism. If you are unable to judge your son, or your father, or your sister, or your mother, or your nearest relative, or best of friends, or those who may dissuade you from judicial responsibilities, ask another judge to help you. There is no shame, for I understand how easily the whispering and manipulative evil that surrounds your house can influence your decision. That is why I am here. To guide you so you may overwhelm and defeat evil. That is My purpose: to endow humanity with a shield of protection against pervasive and influential evil.'

"Follow the roads of justice so you may live to inherit the land which Yehuway your God gives you.

Because Yehuway is ever watchful, desiring always to love you, do not plant a grove of trees near the altar of Yehuway your God. Everyone about it must see it for what it represents: an earthly link to the wonders of heavenly law and mercy.

"Listen again to Yehuway: 'The shade must not blind justice. The tree must not come to represent the symbol of a decision as it will rest beside My own altar of decisions. Trees die. Altars fall and disassemble. Therefore, do not erect a stone pillar because the people will view it as a permanent place for your seat of judgment. All marbled edifices crumble. Anything that interferes with My plan of judicial performance, I, Yehuway, detest.'

"You will not sacrifice to Yehuway your God any bullock, or sheep, that is blemished. Do not ask for anything that others may construe as an evil request against another person. Such a thing is an abomination to Yehuway your God.

"If you find within any of your communities a man or woman who has brought wickedness in the sight of Yehuway your God, by transgressing against His covenant, bring the matter before the courts. It is your responsibility to the community. If either the man or the woman is found to have abandoned the truth of Yehuway to serve other gods in false worship, or makes divinations using the sun, or the moon, or any of the stars of heaven as a magical influence, they are intolerable to Yehuway.

"Listen to Yehuway's decree: 'No, I shall never tolerate or approve such a reference. If someone witnesses about the words of an astrologer or diviner to the Council of Wise Men, you must listen to the accusation. After carefully gathering the evidence, proceed with due diligence. Listen extremely carefully to these types of accusations. The judges must carefully, attentively, and prudently weigh the evidence. Sometimes a diviner's words do not originate from the demons as many false leaders speak just to hear themselves saying something from nothingness. Behold, if the accusation proves true, and it is irrefutable that such an abomination has indeed been practiced in Yisra'el, then you must remove the man or the woman who has committed that wicked thing from your community and petition Yehuway to pass judgment upon the sinner.

"Remember, no man is empowered to harm another man. If Yehuway does not punish the sinner, leave him alone for you are not qualified to hurt the sinner as you yourself are a sinner.

"'From the mouth of a minimum of two witnesses, or better yet, three witnesses, shall the sinner be judged to walk to the throne of Yehuway to be judged by the ultimate judge. If no judgement is enacted, leave the person alone for Yehuway himself is only qualified to pass final sentence. He will do so on his day of retribution.

"Again, I remind you," Mikha'el the Archangel continued to speak Yehuway's laws, "if a judicial difficulty occurs that is too complex for you to make a proper and judicial decision, then seek the advice of an impartial judge. For example, if a conflict between blood and blood, between a plead and a plead, between a stroke and a stroke, becomes an agitated matter of controversy within your gates, then rise up and travel to the nearest location which Yehuway your God shall choose. Travel to the kohanim as well as to the experienced and mature judge who is well respected among the people and who has in that present time great wisdom and maturity. Discuss with them the matter of the judicial violation, so through your inquiry the people will see that you sought out every means of mercy for the accused. The mature and experienced counselors will recommend the sentence of judgment. In that location, in the Seat of Judgment, you must do according to the rendered sentence that they have advised you to carry out. Yehuway has chosen the locale and He has guided you to the proper authorities. Now, observe everything that they have informed you to do. Yes, perform it according to their wisdom. You are now free from a prejudiced decision that might have gone against you in the sight of the people.

"Remember, your task is to pass a judgement, not to execute the sinner. When you render a judicial decision, be sure to perform it with mercy. Weigh the matter with a prudential judgment. That which the kohanim taught you, do. The judgment must stem from the hearts of the righteous. Do not veer toward the right hand or the left. The man that will do so and who refuses to listen to the kohen who stood to minister before Yehuway your God and who disobeys the dictates of the judge, even that man himself shall be judged standing beside the accused. Yehuway alone will dislocate evil from earth.

"Listen to Yehuway: 'Through these proceedings all the people shall hear and understand the mercy of the judgment. Through hearing, they will discern and gain respect for the law's performance, and do nothing badly.

"It has happened that people have called upon Yehuway to establish human rulers over them. Due to their pleads I permitted humans to establish for themselves a human ruler but it will be I, Yehuway your God, who will ultimately pronounce a true ruler over all mankind.

The ultimate ruler I alone shall choose. I will select My son, Yehohshua, as king over you. My chosen king will be born from the Tribe of Judah. The truest king of all, the final king to judge all kings, comes to rule the living eternal physical earth endowed with the powers of law and the righteousness of the holiest of men. His governance is eternal, fashioned after Melchizedek.

"But what is the responsibility of the king? This I say: The designated king must not multiply horses for himself. Nor may he decree or take any action that will cause the people to return to their sinful lifestyles."

Mikha'el the Archangel raised his hands high for effect, "Listen again to Yehuway: 'You must never forsake Yehuway's eternal king. That action is forbidden to you."

"Neither shall the designated king take multiple wives for himself. His heart may turn away from Me and his people as he devotes himself to satisfying the material desires of his multiple wives. Therefore, the designated king should not strive to gain for himself an abundance of silver and gold. Vast materialism is an affront to Me. I will not permit an over abundant lifestyle to My true followers, for My words alone enrich the people's hearts toward salvation. A rich and powerful person leans too far toward evil to come into My salvation. The pursuit of additional wealth distorts the presently rich person toward the pursuits of gold, silver, and marbled edifices. His desires for renown distort My visions and proper guidance. The rich man forgets My laws and decrees in the sea of malice.

"'It shall be, when the designated man is anointed as king over the people, before he can sit upon the throne of his kingdom, he must first write a copy of this law in a book in front of me. I will bear witness to the writing, and I will teach him the meanings of the words. The king must always carry with him the Book of Laws that he himself has inscribed. He must read from it all the days of his life so he may learn to respect and honor Yehuway his God. He must keep all the words of this law and these statutes. On a daily basis, he must perform the truths of the law, in complete obedience with the law. The law is above all men and women and children, as it is above the angels of the heavens, for they also are subjects of the law. The king, more so than the people, is a slave to the law, because he is the fulfiller of the law's task. It is the law that has condemned Adam and therefore all his children. It is the law that shall free Adam's children to live in a world of righteousness, for that is My purpose: to present salvation to the children of the man whom I once dearly loved – for I Myself created human beings from the elements of the earth which I Myself created from My own entity. I alone guide everything that is. I purpose harmony for prosperity and so all may live with Me, the laws are presented to you. If one single being can abide by the law, that being shall stand on My right side.

"'Let the man who stands as king over the people understand first the law so his heart may never become arrogant nor become a betraying influence against Me. The king is not superior to his brethren. The rich man is not superior to his brethren. The king and the influential man must never turn aside from My commandments. Nor must the king or the wealthy man lean neither toward the right hand nor to the left. To this purpose, the designated man who becomes king may prolong his days as he serves Me in the performance of the laws during his tenure as king in this judicial kingdom.'

"Perform righteously so Yehuway may present a kingly foundation and a kingly inheritance for His children in the midst of Yisra'el."

ഇൗരാഇൗരാഇൗരാഇൗരാ

Yehuway speaks to His prophet through Mikha'el the Archangel.

"Again, what is the purpose of the law? What is the prophecy concerning the establishment of the kohanim? It is so I, Yehuway your God may raise from among you the ultimate, final, and truest King-Prophet. Only one man may ever carry upon himself the kohen-king designation. Only he shall eternally establish the Kingdom of Righteousness. Yes, from the very midst of you the ultimate Shiloh—the Mashi'ach—will rise: Shiloh, Unveiled. Yes, from your very own brethren. Exactly as you have listened to Me; so must you also listen to him, for he is the last judge. The ultimate Lawyer-King-Priest combined into a single person. This I will cause to happen because your very mouths called for Me to perform it for your sakes. In mercy toward you, I shall allow it. Remember the words that you had spoken to Moshe at Horeb during the day that I called an assembly of the people. Because your hearts and minds were unable to bear the wonders of My Holy Presence, the sins of your fear caused you to shout to Moshe: 'Let us not hear again the voice of Yehuway our God. Neither let us see this great fire any more as we may die from such a presence.' Thus what you have asked for from Moshe will occur.

"What you have spoken for is that which you have spoken.

"The sins that you have incurred asked for righteous redemption through the graces of innocence. That is why I will raise up the truest and final Prophet from among your brethren. My perfect companion will look exactly as a human being in the form of a male. I will not endow a woman with My powers or with the holdings of anointed office because it was Havva who sinned in front of My eyes, beguiled by the lies of Satan. This first lie influenced Havva into transgression, an open act of rebellion against Me, but because the sin did not originate with her, I will forgive women and place them on an equal footing with man in his earthly life in all matters with the exception of the spiritual priesthood. A woman, however, may speak of Godly matters alongside men with this one rule: she must cover her hair with a veil. She does not have to cover her face or hide her mouth and cheeks from Me, as I already know who she is. However, for the sake of Havva's original transgression, whenever a female approaches the spiritual counsel, she must cover her hair in humiliation and reminder of that moment of transgression against Me. Yes, only during this session, otherwise, the woman is free to permit her hair, face, and cheeks to remain uncovered. After all, the woman is not an inferior person to the man. This "hairdress principal" is an unrighteous dictate by wicked men seeking to enhance their inferior status. Women are also the Children of Yehuway. Women must have an equal education to the male. With equal skills, the woman shall walk alongside man as his helpmate and advisor. Again, only in the spiritual presence of a male and in the designation of kings, must the woman step aside. Never forget the strong abilities and influences that Sarah and Leah held alongside their husbands. Do not so easily dismiss the spiritual strength of the prophetess Miriam. However, only with the male will I place My ultimate spiritual truths. A male heir will rise to be the ultimate ruler of the people. I shall put My words into the ultimate male's mouth, for the Mashi'ach can only be a male just as I am a Male.

"I am not born or created from a woman as no mother gave me birth. It is absolutely impossible for flesh to birth spirit. I am self-created, from My own entity. It cannot even be said that the cosmos created Me, for it is I who created the cosmos. Everything that exists throughout the universe, down to the smallest forms, belongs exclusively to Me. The Ultimate Mashi'ach whom I will transfer from spiritual to flesh so he may be born from a woman is tasked to speak My words to all whom I shall direct him toward. Yet, this miraculous birth does not empower the flesh to rule spirit, for it can never be.

Equality of women with men

"Heaven does not discriminate between men and women, so why should earthlings? Men and women are equal in financial responsibilities, household upkeep, rearing of children, education. Only in centers of worship must the woman take a lower position by wearing a veil over her hair during the religious ceremony. Otherwise, veils are not required, and in fact, a degradation to her husband and family. Only in a place of worship is the woman permitted to cover the top of her hair with a veil. Her eyes and cheeks do not need to be covered.

"Though a woman has full equality with her husband, she is not permitted to hold religious instructions as long as an older male is present in the congregation. Only an older male may speak and teach spiritual matters to th congregation. Never is a woman allowed to present blessed sacraments to the congregation. If no male is present, a simple prayer will suffice, with her hair covered, her form bowed. It shall come to pass whoever denigrates a woman financially, or abuses her physically, or tries to steal from her the inheritance provided to her by her father, is a falsifier of my values toward women.

"Whoever refuses to listen to My words which the true and final Mashi'ach speaks in My name, I Myself will call that person to an accounting: both male and female.

Beware Charismatic Preachers

"I know, though, that many will attempt to deceive you away from Me with beguiling words and with a charismatic presence. The demons know how to trick the innocent away from Me. They will consume the innocents with hatred by presenting to them everything that seems kind and favorable with easy things to listen to. Cunning music filled with harmonic rhymes are in truth filled with an underlying message of deceit. Only I can decree for men to war against other men: in all cases only to protect and enhance the survival of the innocent ones.

"The demons will also speak words to create false governments that seem to be under the care and protection of My name, but indeed they are set against Me. How many will say 'Country under God,' but in reality it is a 'Country under Satan'! Remember, all governments outside Yisra'el are under the control of a deceitful evil who intends to destroy humanity. Already have I pronounced the sentence of justice against the evil workers. Do not be among them. I have not recorded their names and faces in advance because free choice is not a destined force. Nevertheless, this judgment applies not to predetermined evildoers, but to the evildoers who have not yet awakened from their mother's wombs. The sinner knows he is a sinner. The sinner can pray and work toward good things. He may yet gain a bestowment of My kind graces upon himself. I want to share My grace with everyone on the earth. I do not desire to limit it. However, because the witnesses of the acts of iniquity call their names out, I must listen to them. The persons, through the acts of their witnessed evil, intend to take into Sheol as many as they can to spite My Name and Holy Presence. I purpose otherwise, but the witnesses demand vengeance. They lack the mercy that I desire to share among all. Remember, all men are gifted with the ability to choose their paths, for no man's feet are set into an inescapable path. I, Yehuway, hate a man of destiny, for who is destined to perform what? I alone purpose things, and there is not one human being ever, at any time, who has been created without the ability to go either to the right, or to the left, or to the forefront and rear of the road.

"For this reason, beware the false prophet who presumes to speak words in My name. Truly, I have not commanded him to speak. If a man pretends to be a prophet and dares to speak in the name of other gods, that false prophet must die. He speaks through evil and deceitful Satan. If you say in your heart, 'How are we to know the words which Yehuway has not spoken?' This is the answer: When a prophet speaks in the name of Yehuway, if what he declares does not happen, nor those things come to pass, then that is the thing which Yehuway has not spoken. It is a lie. When the pretender and false prophet speaks beyond the bounds, do not be afraid of him. He is a liar. A man who seeks his own virtue is a selfish man ambitious for wealth, power, and fame. With every moment's breath, he asks you for your donation as he covers his true intent with beautiful and compelling messages of hope and life in the heavens under good governance. But where is the paradise for mankind? Surely, not beside Me, for what man is so pure? I alone am able to place my fingertip on his chest and I alone can transform his human body to a spiritual body able to withstand the power and dignity of My throne. There is no rapture or mystical callings or magical transformation through the voices of the false prophets. I will discover the man and woman and child whom I alone want. They will never boast of this gift, for it is a burdensome gift. A calling to Godly work requires extreme compassion. The workers of mercy are my children, but the workers of evil will be condemned to an eternal forgottenness. The workers of mercy will be the teachers of the light, empowered with all things wonderful to help the remainder of mankind to live on this earth which I originally created to be mankind's physical paradise. Only the spiritually qualified whom I alone designate will enter the gates of My heavenly abode. The remainder will stay settled on the wondrous earth that I have created for them. Make no mistake about this. The number is 12 times 12 according to the creative spans that I formed the universe."

അതഃഅതഃഅതഃഅതഃഅതഃ

Mikha'el the Archangel speaks:

Property Rights

"Do not remove your neighbor's landmark. They are provided from the first settlement of the land to become an inheritance for the Children of Abraham. What land you inherit, Yehuway your God has provided it as a gift to you.

"Remember, one witness shall not rise up against a man for any iniquity, or for any sin. In any sin that a man or a woman commits, the mouths of two witnesses, or the mouths of three must witness and testify to the sin's commission with non-disputable verification. If a false witness rises up against a man or a woman and presents a false testimony against another man or woman, then both persons shall stand before Yehuway and before the kohanim and the judges. They will handle the matter before the righteous and ultimate Judge. The judges, to assure the righteousness of the case, must make diligent inquisition—and, behold—if the witness is a false witness and has testified falsely against his brother or sister, then you must do to him what he had thought to have done to his brother or sister. Through this manner you will dislodge the evil away from you. Those who remain, shall hear, and fear, and shall henceforth commit no more evil acts among you. Your eye must not pity the person receiving the punishment. A life-taker shall forfeit his life, as well as an eye for an eye, a tooth for a tooth, a hand for a hand, a foot for a foot. Whoever enacts a malice act against another, in turn, will suffer the identical malice act upon himself.

"This law must be adhered to as evidence of your willingness to equate sin for sin until the coming of the ultimate law-performer: he who is the fulfiller of the law: The Ultimate Mashi'ach.

The Mashi'ach of Mashi'achs."

ಬಇಚ3ಬಇಚ3ಬಇಚ3ಚಇಬಇಚ3ಬಇಚ3

CHAPTER

7

MIKHA'EL THE ARCHANGEL SPEAKS:

"I cannot stress enough to you enough that each day you will encounter a rigorous and demonic challenge. That is why I am now preparing your hearts and minds with the declarations of the law and the processes of government to protect you from the evildoers. Permit Yehuway's laws to be your fortress and shield against the false one.

Conscientious Objectors

"In ancient days, prior to My son's fleshy appearance on earth it was said of Yisra'el's armed forces, 'When you send your armies against your enemies, and when you see a great quantity of horses and chariots accompanied by a vast number of foot soldiers and armaments, do not be afraid of them. Do not panic for Yehuway your God is with you: the very same God who brought you out of the land of prejudiced and scornful Egypt where you were an afflicted race of hated aliens. Prior to engaging the enemy in battle—a Levite kohen—must first approach me and speak on the people's behalf but that requirement has been set aside for my only begotten son has already fulfilled the covenant between him and I, between mankind and myself.

" 'Today, reveal to the treacherous the crime they are about to perpetrate against you. When you approach your enemies who battle against you, do not permit your hearts to panic! Have no fear! Do not tremble nor become terrified! Yehuway your God stands beside you to settle your fears.

" 'In the times of Joshua and King David, and King Josiah, though I routed the enemies' offense and increased my children's defenses, and increased their maneuvers to overwhelm their fortifications, that is no longer the way I will conduct warfare on my children's behalf.

" 'My only begotten son has paid the price of his fleshly life to preserve mankind. My intervention is no longer necessary. I hold my wrath until my own declared Day of Finality for the wars of mankind.

"No government should humiliate the peaceful man. No one should shame the retreating man. They are not cowards. They are blessed with a higher calling to the importance of life. No man is permitted to brand the refuser to carry arms in a demeaning fashion. The man who refuses to fight is a righteous man, filled with a purified heart who cannot bear to render harm to another fellow human being.

" 'Each officer is obligated to ask every one of his soldiers prior to a battle: 'What man among you has recently built a new house that has not yet been dedicated? Today, the law's mercy releases you from this battle. Go without shame or regret and without condemnation. Return to your house, lest by circumstance and misfortune a bullet or a bomb or a knife or a stone or a tank's cannon may make its mark upon you, and you perish from the blow. Another man must not be permitted to dedicate your house unto himself. What you have established, you must enjoy, for life is brief under this system of things.'

"The officer must continue inquiring of his men. He must also ask, 'What man now present among you has recently planted a vineyard and has not yet eaten from it? That man may also leave the battle without shame or repudiation. Return to your house, lest you die in the battle and another man enjoy your vineyard. It is not proper for such a thing to happen, for what you planted must first be consumed by you, for it was through your efforts that the fruit was brought forth to quench your own thirst and satisfy your hunger.'

"Also, let the officer ask: 'What man here has just betrothed a wife and has yet to enjoy the sexual pleasures of the marriage? Return to your house, lest you die in the battle and another man wed her and take her into his own arms to engage in sexual intercourse with her. She, though briefly, is the happiness of your heart under this system of things.'

"Then, with a careful and quiet voice, with a voice of compassionate understanding, the officer must further ask the soldiers: 'What man here is fearful and fainthearted? If you are afraid of the coming battle, please return to your house, lest your own fear ripple throughout the camp and your brethren's heart become infected with just as great a faint as your own.' It is better to let the man who is afraid to return to his house where he can dwell within the security of his family and land rather than to swell the ranks with doubt. Betrayal can result and the battle lost. Do not repudiate or hold in shame the man who leaves the battle as his heart calls for peace. He is not a coward nor be branded as a coward. He is a conscientious objector to war, and for such, must be respected for what he is.

"Frown against abusing the man who will not fight. It has no place in my righteous affairs.

"I, alone, will designate the final battle's conclusion. All wars that occurred between the period of my only begotten's rising from the Tomb of Death until my day of Vengeance are wars led by satanic influence. I will not demand a battle to take place upon the earth led by humans for the prophecies concerning by son have been fulfilled. "I, alone, will vanquish evil from the earth,. I, Yehuway, will reinforce my laws with a new vigorous army composed of angels. They will become my designated executioners of sinners for no man is qualified to kill another man.

"No armies shall ever exist comprised of human beings.

"A different type of warfare will take place on Yehuway's Day of Retribution. Earth is determined for His righteous believers. In the times of Judgement his anointed will be empowered to convert all people to a single religion. Yehuway's extermination of sinners will cease as soon as the people accept his righteous decrees and accept his provisions to live in a land of exquisite charm and magnitude. After the righteous have settled themselves in paradise, a time of sharing will arise.

"When Yehuway's righteous army, composed strictly from his seraphims, approaches earth the residents will be offered an opportunity to surrender themselves to his angels without molestation. If the sinner accepts Yehuway and lives according to his laws and never forsake their allegiance to him, they shall live in peace upon earth's continents.

"Listen to Yehuway's words: 'If the person who converts later refuses to obey the laws he will perish at the hands of the designated angels of Yehuway. No human being may ever harm another human being. My wrath, on the completion of my vengeance, will refrain me from further warfare for no one will ever again challenge my sovereignty.'

"The destruction of sinners will signify to the world that the true God is devoted to sanctification and vindication of earth as well as to His name. 'I will gift all human beings my mercy so the conquered will learn who I am. The conquered may have yet a chance to embrace Me into their hearts. Creating for them a path for their salvation into righteousness.

"'If the citizens refuse to negotiate a peaceful treaty with me, and I do indeed find them unacceptable, then I will wage a war of total annihilation against them. I will besiege the citizens for they are evildoers. They have taken up false residence in the land of righteousness. After I, Yehuway your God, have delivered the citizenry into the hands of my vindictive angels, they will be empowered to slaughter every male with the edge of the bronze tipped sickle-sword. I will instruct them not to refrain, as I, Yehuway, demand it to be so. I will commission my angels to this task so men may see how I can invigorate justice to such a heightened power. One angel is capable of killing a quarter million fully armed men. Not one of My true enemies will remain alive. I will empower my angel to destroy all opposers without hesitation: the old men, the young men, as well as the male children who are yet weaning.

"'However, I will make a provision for the human beings who express regret, even on the final second of my retribution if they but ask for mercy. I will permit the sinners, on their sincere plead, to eat to their full contentment from the fruit trees and vegetable gardens which grow abundantly in paradise.

"I am Yehuway your God.

"However, the sinners, filled to capacity in their hearts with sin, will not ask me for mercy. They are incapable of uttering such a simple plead. They will defile my warrior angels and spit in their faces and try to scar their cheeks with drawn knifes. The power brokers are treacherous. Therefore, my angels must exterminate them. Do not have compassion for the former leaders. They are treacherous.

"My paradise, my decrees, I gift to the righteous. Learn them and keep them in your heart even in the remote fringes of your settlements. What land I give to you becomes yours to present as an inheritance to your children. Yehuway your God permits it to become so. The lands that you settle into shall remain with you. What you have been given, keep for yourselves. Do not surrender to anyone the land that you have gained.

"Remember, in the age before peace finally came to earth, the Gazans, the enemy of Israel, tasked them to return to them the land which the Jews conquered in 1973 so they could peacefully live beside their enemies. Remember, there is no such thing as peace for land. What you have gained, I presented it to you. Hold on to it. Build your houses on the land and enrich it with crops. Flourish in the land It is I who gifted you with the land.

"When you reside in paradise, do not mourn for those relatives who failed to convert to righteousness.

"They waged war against Me, and I in turn I waged war against them. Who is so distant that I cannot reach them? Who can bury themselves so deep that I cannot dig them out? Therefore, be at comfort with what I had to do. I instructed my minions to kill everything on the sin filled earth: men, and, yes, when directed, even the women and the children. Do not mourn for the children as it is the parents who impregnated their minds with bitter hatred against the righteous. Even the remote territories that are populated with a people you are unlikely ever to see must also become void of the trespassers. They are not the Children of earth. Never again shall I allow an unrighteous person to trespass earth. I will destroy them. Time and distance have no meaning for Me. Today my enemies are the demons as well as those who follow them. After the Day of Vengeance, I shall never again have an enemy.

"Those who had fermented deep and grave hostility against the righteous will no longer exist. Those who followed satanic paths will no longer exist. I have sanctified the earth just as I, Yehuway your God, have foreseen it.

"In centuries to come the survivors will learn why I executed the sinners who had filled the earth. Never again will any human face the abominations which evil had presented to tempt them away from me. In return for my gift of life, all humans who survived my wrath must pledge to me never to permit themselves to be influenced toward the practices of evil ways and lean against my laws, or perform the things they had performed toward false gods and ambitions. To do so is to sin against me, Yehuway your God. It will not be permitted. Not even for a single moment.

৪৩৪৫৪৩৪৫৪৩৫৫৪৩৪৫

CHAPTER

8

MIKHA'EL THE ARCHANGEL REFLECTS on Yehuway's laws prior to 2016. Laws spoken to Moshe, based on the needs of presenting through the line of David a genetically pure birth – the Messiah of Yisra'el.

"A time once existed when laws were provided to the Children of Abraham to protect them from foreign intervention, false accusations, and punishment of the innocent.

"If by chance a slain person is discovered in the fields in the land that Yehuway your God gave to you to own, and it is not known who had slain him, then your elders and your judges must come forth and measure from the spot where the slain body is discovered to the surrounding villages of the corpse. The elders of the village that is nearest to the slain man must take a heifer that has never pulled a yoke nor worked in the field. The elders of that city shall lead the heifer to a torrent wadi that has not been tilled or sown. A kohen must walk in front of the elders as it must be the Levite's responsibility to perform the killing of the heifer. They are the ones whom Yehuway your God have chosen to minister and to bless you in the name of Yehuway. In front of the villagers and the owners of the fields and in front of the elders, in the center of that wadi, the kohen must break the neck of the heifer in the valley.

"Through this very method the kohanim—the sons of Levi—will offer the young cow as settlement of the unverifiable crime. Through Levitical interpretation, every dispute and every violent act will be handled with reference to the law. All the counselors of the village who are near the slain person must wash their hands over the heifer whose neck was broken in the valley of flowing waters. Together, in unison, with the kohanim leading the words, the elders shall repeat these words: 'Our hands have not shed this blood, neither have our eyes seen it. Be merciful, Yehuway, to your people Yisra'el, whom you have redeemed, and lay not innocent blood on your people of Yisra'el's charge.' The victim's blood will not hold hostage that village as recompense for an unsolved crime. The villagers are innocent.

"In this manner you will send away the guilt of innocent blood from among you, when you perform the thing that is right in the sight of Yehuway.

"When you engage in battle against your enemies, and Yehuway your God has delivered them into your hands as captives, if you happen to discover a beautiful woman among the prisoners and desire to have sex with her, she must first become your wife. You will not rape her! You will not sexually assault her or demean her in any manner whatsoever! This is how you must treat the female prisoner. If you desire her for your bed, you must first wed the female prisoner. After the wedding, bring her to your house where she shall shave her head and pare her nails. She shall remove the clothing of her captivity from her body and dress herself with the new clothing of her new life. In the first full month that she remains in your house permit her to freely mourn for her father and her mother. After the full month of mourning passes, after her grief is spent and she becomes accustomed to your house and friends and family, present her to the kohanim for spiritual training in the ways of Yehuway for thirty days. Only after two months of her presence in your tent may you have sexual intercourse with her, for you will have been married as husband and wife for two full months. Should it happen, however, that she is not as you had expected her to be and that she refuses to accept your family and friends and abide by the culture of Yisra'el and refuses to surrender herself to devotion to Yehuway, release her to go wherever she wants. Do not sell her for any amount of money! Do not make her into a piece of merchandise because you have already humiliated her.

"In this manner must a husband address the issue of two wives. If a man has two wives, and he loves one more than he loves the other, and both of them bear him children, both the beloved as well as the hated, and the firstborn son belongs to the wife whom the husband hates, then divide the land through this method. The husband who is the father of the son must not favorably give to the son of the beloved firstborn before the son of the hated, who is indeed the true firstborn. Rather, the father must acknowledge the son of the hated wife as his genuine firstborn. He must give to him a double portion of all that he has – for he is the beginning of his strength. This is the right of the firstborn whether through a favored wife or a despised wife.

"In this manner, deal with a rebellious child. If a man has a stubborn and rebellious son who will not obey his father's voice or the voice of his mother, then do this. First, discipline him. If he still does not listen to the parents, then his father and his mother must grab him and bring him to the counselors of the village – yes, to the very gate of the place where they live. They shall inform the leaders of the village, 'This is our son. He is stubborn and rebellious. He will not obey our voice. He is a glutton and a drunkard.'

"After this testimony of the two parents all the men of the village will be called together to stone the disobedient son with stones, striking him with a rapid volley until he perishes. In this manner, you must remove the demonic evil away from you. Let all Yisra'el hear of the disobedient son's death so other children working toward bad deeds may circumvent their bad behavior and respect the law.

"If a man commits a sin worthy of death and he is hung on a stake until his life force leaves him as a corpse, do not permit his body to remain all night long upon that stake. You should quickly bury him before the sunset of that very same day, for an impaled person on that single beam becomes a malediction to God. Why should the eyes of the Righteous Creator see him any more than He has to? Perform the burial so your land may not be defiled which Yehuway your God give you for an inheritance."

ಬಂ೮ಽ ಬಂ೮ಽ ಬಂ೮ಽಽ ಬಂ೮ಽ

"If a dispute breaks out between two men, and they have presented themselves before the judges for the judges to proscribe punishment or innocence; then they shall justify the righteous, and condemn the wicked. If it happens that the guilty person deserves to be punished by a lash, the law-enforcer shall cause him to lie down and be beaten in front of his face, according to the degree of the guilt's satisfaction. It may be 1 lash, 3 lashes, 5 lashes, 10, 15, 25, or 30 – but never more than

40 lashes. To exceed forty lashes is the same as to degrade the guilty person beyond the scope of the crime. Do not lash the person so harshly and so mercilessly that the offender will die. The crime, if it warrants death, calls then for stoning, not lashings. The lashing is an example to bear witness to the crime. Why make this thing become a vile act for you?

"You must not muzzle the ox while it is threshing.

"If by circumstances two brothers live together in the same house, and one of them should die without having fathered a child, the wife of the dead brother shall not marry a stranger. Her husband's brother shall marry her and then have sexual intercourse with her. When she gives birth to the firstborn, that child shall succeed in the name of his brother who had perished. Yehuway grants this mercy so the family name may endure in the annals of Yisra'el. If it happens that the living brother refuses to marry his brother's wife, then permit his brother's wife to walk to the gate of the tribal leaders and say, 'My husband's brother refuses to marry me and impregnate me with an heir to my husband's name. His name and his properties will not be able to be passed on to an heir in Yisra'el. His living brother chastises me, leaving me as a virgin in my own house. Yes, he refuses to marry me so we may have sexual intercourse to produce an inheritor for his brother's sake.'

"After this testimony the leaders of the town must visit the living brother to speak to him the reasons concerning the inheritance and the passing on of the family's name and inheritance. With full diligence, the elders of the council must try to persuade the living brother to perform the just marriage with the expected sexual intercourse to produce a child in the living wife's womb. If the living brother stands to his decision and still refuses to marry the dead brother's wife, he must say to the elders, 'I do not want her as my wife. I do not want to have sexual intercourse with her.' After this, his brother's wife must walk to him in the presence of the leaders and remove his shoe from his foot. She must spit in his face, and say, 'So shall it be done to that man who will not build up his brother's house.' And his name shall be called in Yisra'el, 'This is house of he who has had his shoe unlaced.'

"If two men get into a brawl with each other, and the wife of the one of those fighters comes near them so she can save her husband from the other fighter, and in doing so, grabs the other man's testicles and squeezes them harshly, regardless of her intent to help her husband, her hand must be amputated. Your eyes shall not pity her.

"You must not carry in your trading bag various weights of measure: a heavy one and a light one, to serve as manipulators of the trade. Nor must you have in your house deceiving weights of measure so you may gain an unfavorable advantage over the buyer. Indeed, you must maintain a perfect and just weight of measure for all your transactions with all of your customers so your days may be lengthened in the land which Yehuway your God give you.

"For all those who do such things, and for all those who work through schemes and manipulations, these very same people are an abomination to Yehuway your God.

"Never forget the terrible injustice that Amalek did against you as you traveled on the paths to this land from Egypt. Do not ever forget how they ignored your pains and sufferings that you underwent in that land as an afflicted race of hated aliens. Do not forget how those audacious and treacherous military personnel met you on the roadside and how they proceeded to murder your old men and pregnant women who marched in the rear. Yes, they did not care how feeble and faint and weary they were. Without mercy, they slaughtered and plundered the helpless people seeking solitude in a land of righteousness. The abusers did not respect or honor God.

"Thus, it must be, even after Yehuway your God permit you to rest from the tribulations of all your enemies who surround you throughout the land that Yehuway your God, give you for an inheritance to possess, you should continue your quest to blot out the remembrance of Amalek from under heaven. Do not forget it. Annihilate and eradicate them: they, and their heirs, and their children's children, even throughout the generations. Yes, eradicate the evildoers from the face of the earth before their malice afflicts you with grief and ruination. This is a divine decree. Perform it to its utter and total completion."

೮೦೮೩೮೦೮೩೮೦೮೩೮೦೮೩೮೦೮೩

Mikha'el the Archangel speaks Yehuway's decrees to the people of Moshe's era:

"If by chance you happen to catch sight of your brother's ox or his sheep going astray, do not hide yourself from them. Do not take another path away from the problem. Under all circumstances, you must do your best to capture them and return them back to your brother. If your brother is not nearby, or if you do not know where he is, then take the ox or sheep to your own house. Permit them to remain with you until your brother misses them and seeks their whereabouts. Ease his fears in the loss of his possessions by restoring them back to him.

"In similar manner, do the same thing with his donkey. Again, do not stop with the kindness just concerning his animals. Do exactly the same thing with his outer wool coat as well as with all the lost thing of your brother's. Whatever he has lost, whatever you have found that does not belong to you, return it to the owner. Never hide yourself from performing this task. It is not his problem alone. It is the problem of everyone in the world. To keep what is lost is the same as stealing it.

"The same thing must be applied if your brother's donkey or ox happens to trip and fall down alongside the roads and byways. Do not hide yourself from them. Do not take another path away from the problem. You should make every effort possible to help lift the animals up again."

ಖಿ‍ೕಖಿ‍ೕಖಿ‍ೕಖಿ‍ೕ

"A woman should not wear a man's clothes. Neither should a man wear women's clothing. All who do so are an abomination to Me, Yehuway your God."

ಖಿ‍ೕಖಿ‍ೕಖಿ‍ೕಖಿ‍ೕ

"If a bird's nest happens to be built on the branches that you need to work on, or if the bird's nest happens to be built on the ground that you are tilling, or if the eggs hatch and young ones are born within that nest, or you happen upon a female bird nestling her eggs, do not destroy it. Remove the dam with her young to another location. If the dam attacks you, leave her and the nest where it is. However, if it is necessary to remove the nestling, permit the dam to live. Do not kill her. Take her young ones with you to your own home and raise them properly so it may be well with you and so you may prolong your days. The birds are the descendants of a great life that once inhabited the earth long before you."

ಐಲ3ಐಲ3ಐಲ8ಐಲ3ಐಲ3

"When you build a new house, extend the roof line with a surrounding battlement. If a visitor or relative happens to fall asleep on your roof, or walks and trips and falls from your roof, the extension should be able to catch that person. Through this protective device you will not bring blood upon your house if any person falls from the roof."

ಐಲ3ಐಲ3ಐಲ8ಐಲ3ಐಲ3

"Do not sow your vineyard with various seeds, lest the fruit that matures from your planted seed, as well as the fruit of your vineyard, becomes defiled. Through your laziness and neglect, you may cause corruption among the pollinators.

"Do not plow the fields of the farm land with an ox and a donkey lassoed together. Do not mingle their excrement.

"Do not wear clothing sown from various threads, such as a mixture and blending of wool and linen together. Extend the fringes of your pure clothing four quarters beyond the final binding of the vesture which you intend to wear."

"If any man takes a wife for himself, and after having sexual intercourse with her hates her, and afterward makes occasional abusive speech against her, even to the point of embarrassing her and brings an evil name upon her, he should publicly declare: 'After I married this woman and had sex with her I discovered she was not a virgin.' Then the father of the damsel as well as her mother should take the marital beddings of the night that they had spent together as evidence of the damsel's virginity before the marital consummation. Present the stained sheets of the ruptured hymen to the elders of the village that stand by the gate. The damsel's father shall say to the elders, 'I gave my daughter to wed this man, and now he hates her. Look! Occasionally he speaks abusive things about her. He said, "I found out that your daughter is not a virgin." Yet here are the tokens of my daughter's virginity.'

"The parents of the daughter shall spread the cloth of the marriage night before the elders of the city so they may see that the hymen ruptured: her virginity properly surrendered to the man she wed. Then the elders of that city shall take that man and publicly chastise him. The abusive husband must pay a fine of one hundred shekels of silver to the father of the damsel because he has placed a false rumor against a virgin of Yisra'el. She shall remain his wife. However, under no circumstances may the husband remove her from his house for the rest of the days of his life. However, if she indeed was not a virgin on their wedding night, and the stains of virginity are not discovered as evidence for the damsel's plea, then the judges must bring the damsel to the door of her father's house. In front of him, the men of the city will stone her with stones until she perishes from the blows, because she has brought folly into Yisra'el. She plays the whore in her father's house! Remove this evil away from among you.

"Moreover, if a man is caught having sex with a married woman, both adulterers must perish. Yes, both of them, the adulterous man who had sex with the woman, as well as the adulterous woman must appear before the judges. Remove this evil away from Yisra'el.

"If a virgin damsel becomes betrothed to a future husband, then another man meets her as she is walking by him in the private and remote streets of the city, and he persuades her to have sex with him, then you must bring both of them to the city gate. There, you shall stone both of them with a swift volley of stones until they perish from the blows. Do this because the damsel failed to cry out in her defense. She resides in an area where there are multitudes of people about her. Also, the false perpetrator humbled his neighbor's wife. Remove away this evil from among you.

"However, if a man finds a betrothed damsel in the field and rapes her, then sentence to death the rapist. Do not harm the damsel, however. Do nothing against her! She has done nothing worthy of death. The sin visited upon her was not her fault. This is the same as when a man rises against his neighbor and slays him!

Even so is this matter: for the rapist met her in the field, either through chance or deliberately, and the betrothed damsel cried out, yet none saved her.

"In the case where a man finds a damsel who is a virgin—who is not betrothed—and has sexual intercourse with her, and they are discovered, then the man who had sex with her shall give to the damsel's father fifty shekels of silver. Moreover, she shall become his wife. Because he has humbled her, he may not divorce her for the rest of the days of his life.

"In addition to all these things concerning sexual intercourse—voluntary and involuntary—note this: a son may never have sexual intercourse with his father's wife, whether she is divorced or whether he has perished. To do so is the same as to uncover his father's skirt. Your penis may never substitute for your father's penis. Your erection may never penetrate the identical vagina that he had formerly enjoyed."

ೞღೞღೞღೞღೞღ

"The man who has suffered a severe blow to his testicles, crushing them to the point of impotence, either through the fling of stones or through the striking of a bat, or through a harsh fall from a tree, cannot enter into the congregation of Yehuway. The same will be true for the man whose penis is cut off. The pride of the emission of semen into his wife's vagina, unfortunately, is lost for the castrated man and eunuch. Moreover, an illegitimate person can never enter into the congregation of Yehuway. Yes, even to the tenth generation (five hundred years, or, half a spiritual day) his descendants cannot enter into the congregation of Yehuway."

Yehuway speaks through His only begotten son, Mikha'el the Archangel:

"'An Ammonite or Moabite is also forbidden to enter into the congregation of Yehuway. Yes, even to their tenth generation (five hundred years, or, half a spiritual day) they cannot enter into the congregation of Yehuway. The reason for this banishment is this: they failed to provide you with bread and water as you traveled through the highways when you left scornful Egypt where you lived as an afflicted race of hated aliens. Instead of providing compassionate help, they hired Balaam the son of Beor, from the residence of Pethor of Aram-naharaim, to curse you. Nevertheless, I, Yehuway your God, would not listen to Balaam. I, Yehuway your God, reversed his curse into a blessing for you, because I, Yehuway your God, love you. You will not seek their peace nor make any sort of alliances with them, nor long to foster their prosperity among yourselves as long as you shall live – even unto eternity.

"'In direct contrast to this, you should not abhor an Edomite. He is your brother. Moreover, contrary to what you may believe, you should not abhor an Egyptian, even though you were once an afflicted race of aliens in his land. Think, the Egyptians, for all their abuses and hatreds and scowlings, nevertheless still took care of you. You remained under their protection until you were nurtured enough to leave his land. You went into his land few in number and emerged from his land by the millions! Indeed, it is true! The children who are born to the Egyptians may freely enter the congregation of Yehuway. This will happen in the third generation: or, one hundred seventy years from now as

160

forty years have already passed as you journeyed in the wilderness. Time passes by so rapidly, you blink, and the time is already here.'"

"'When your military power marches against your enemies, refrain from engaging in wicked things.

"'If it happens that a young man's penis swells and erupts with spurts of semen inside his clothes and the semen clings to the inner thighs of his skin due to having dreams of a nocturnal voyage, he must vacate the encampment. He cannot return to the encampment during the morning and even unto late afternoon. During the new twilight, as the earth completes its rotation, the man must have washed his penis and the inner thighs of his skin as well as his clothing with fresh water. When the sun has set, he may again enter the encampment. Wash away the sin of the night's visit with purified water.

"'Furthermore, you must provide for your soldiers and personnel a toilet facility far, far away from the populace where you can release your urine and fecal matter. You should always carry a small shovel alongside your weapon so when you need to defecate, you are able to dig a hole for your usage. When you are finished defecating, turn around to see where you have relieved yourself. Then bury the waste matter that came out from your intestines. You must do this because I, Yehuway your God, constantly walk in the midst of your camp to protect you from your enemies. The feet of an angel must never step into your filthy shit! Therefore, your encampment should become a purified encampment. See to it that only clean things remain within the fortress of your salvation. Otherwise, I, Yehuway, may turn away from you and My angels think badly of you. Your enemies can walk on their own shit and the helms of their garments can drag into the cesspools of urine, but it must not be so with you!'"

ಬಿಂಛಬಿಂಛಬಿಂಛಬಿಂಛಬಿಂಛ

"You are not permitted to force a refugee who has escaped the tyranny of his former back. Instead, permit the refugee to live among you. Yes, among your own relatives and neighbors. Allow him free exploration of the village without hindrance or chastisement, even to the far reaches of your gates. In fact, the gates may be the very place that presents to the runaway slave the best comfort. It can act as his public testimony that the village is safe for him and that he will have juridical protection. Do not oppress the refugee as he is seeking his freedom just as you sought your own freedom from the prejudiced enslavers. The Children of Ham were the first enslavers, followed by the Children of Japheth. Why should the Children of Shem follow their footsteps?"

ಬಿಂಛಬಿಂಛಬಿಂಛಬಿಂಛಬಿಂಛ

"No woman should never serve as a prostitute. The daughters of Yisra'el should never fall on their knees to suck dick or lay on their backs with spread legs and an open vagina to receive an erection for the sake of gaining money to build buildings and adorn temples and provide food and clothing for the false man and false lifestyle. This is why Molech is a detestable god! Nor must a male child, or a teenager or a young male

162

adult, or an older male, ever become a practicer of homosexual acts among the sons of Yisra'el. A sodomite cannot dwell among the people of Yisra'el. An Israelite male of any age must never fall on his knees to suck another male's penis. A man must never have rectal intercourse with another man. No semen may eject from one man's hands into another man's hands. A male must never use his rectum as a vagina for another man. A male may not use his body as a sexual vessel for the enrichment of a religious temple. A man cannot marry another man.

"A woman cannot marry another woman. A mother may never suck her son's penis nor may a son suck his mother's vagina. A father may not suck his son's penis or a son his father's penis. Neither should use they use each other's rectum as a vagina.

"You may never contribute as a tithing the sum of a whore's wage, or the price to purchase a dog, as a gift to the House of Yehuway your God for any vow. Both types of offering are abominations to Yehuway your God. So, if a prostitute costs such and such to do such and such and the price of a dog is such and such – that is the amount that is forbidden to present to Yehuway.

"You should not lend money to your brother with the expectation of an additional usury. Do not practice the usury of money or the usury of victuals or the usury of anything for usury's sake. However, you may lend with interest to a non-Israelite—but never to your brother—so I, Yehuway your God, may bless you in all that you set your hand to in the land that you are about to possess.

"When you pledge a vow with another vow to Yehuway your God, do not hesitate to pay it back. Yehuway your God, surely requires it from you. It would be sin for you not to repay what you have pledged to repay. It is not only a contractual obligation between the borrower and the debtor, it is an obligation with Yehuway's name attached to the contract. However, if you make a pledge without a making an additional vow, it will not become a sin against you. Still, remember, that when your lips speak a promise, you should keep and perform it; even if it is a freewill offering, according as you have vowed to Yehuway your God, whom you have promised with your very own mouth."

ಬಂಙ಄ಬಂಙ಄ಬಂಙ಄ಬಂಙ಄ಬಂಙ಄

"When you enter your neighbor's vineyard and eat the grapes that freely grow on the soil, you may do so without payment to the owner, however, you are not permitted to take any more than you can eat. Do not fill your sack or basket with the owner's possession. Similarly, when you enter your neighbor's wheat and barley fields, pluck the ears only with your hand; but you are not permitted to put a sickle to your neighbor's grain.

ಬಂಙ಄ಬಂಙ಄ಬಂಙ಄ಬಂಙ಄ಬಂಙ಄

"When a man agrees to take a wife for himself, then marries her, and it comes to pass that he does not find her suitable in his eyes (perhaps because he has discovered something unclean about her) then he may write to her a Divorce Bill. He should place it in her hand and send her out of his house. After she has departed from his house, she may become another man's wife. Yet, this must also hold true: the former husband who divorced her and wrote her a Bill of Divorcement, and placed it in her hand, and sent her out of his house, may not remarry her. This is true even if the replacement husband, who had taken her to become his wife, dies. Once her former husband sent her away, he may not take her again as his wife. The back and forth action will cause her to have two men; one a former rejecter, and the other a rejecter through death or banishment. Either way, the woman becomes defiled, similar to a whore. This is an abomination before Yehuway. You must not cause the land to sin, which Yehuway your God, gives to you as an inheritance for your children.

"After a man has married, he should not go to war. Neither should he engage with any business. Instead, he should remain free, staying at home, at least for the first year so he may cheer his wife whom he has married."

ဆဟဂဆဟဂဆဟဂၟဆဟဂဆဟဂ

"No man shall take the nether or the upper millstone as a pledge: for he takes a man's means of earning a living as a pledge."

ဆဟဂဆဟဂဆၟဂဆဟဂဆဟဂ

"If a man is discovered in the act of kidnapping any of his brethren to enslave that person, or to sell that person, then that thief shall die. You must remove all evil away from among you."

"Use caution when you treat those who suffer with skin diseases such as leprosy. Observe diligently their status. Perform everything that you can during the treatment stages according to everything that the Levite kohen taught you. Remember, the kohanim have years of practicing their medical skills as I have instructed them. Do not forget what I, Yehuway your God, did to Miriam during her journey after she had left Egypt because of her rebellion and insubordination against Moshe, her brother."

ဢၢჂဢၢჂဢၢჂ

"When you lend your brother an item, you should not enter his house to fetch the item you had lent him. Instead, you should stand outside the house and wait for the man to whom you lent the item. Permit him on his own accord to bring to you the item from the interior of his house. Let the item become like a pledge of trust between you.

"If the man or woman is poor, and they hand to you their protective garments against the night's cold weather, do not keep that item in your possession overnight so you might avert a catastrophe. In this case, return to that person the pledged item as the sun is going down so that person may sleep in his own raiment. They will bless you. It shall become a righteous act for you before Yehuway your God.

ဢၢჂဢၢჂဢၢჂ

"You should never oppress a hired servant who is poor and needy, whether he is your own brethren, or is among the foreigners who are in your land and within your gates. At the end of his work day, pay that person what he has earned. The sun should not set before he is paid what he has earned. Remember, he is a poor person, and he has expectations for his wage. His heart is set upon it. Do not cheat the worker, lest the worker cry out against you to Me, Yehuway. It is a sin to cheat the worker from his rightful wage."

ಬಂ

"The parents of a sinful child must be punished to the death for the crimes of their children. Similarly, kill the child for the crimes of their parents. Every person should face the consequences of their criminal actions: yes, even if it is death.

"Do not subvert the judicial protections that are in place for you. The foreigners who traverse through your land are also under the protection of My laws. Do not take unfair advantage of those who lost the protection of their parents and became orphans. Do not accept a widow's raiment as a pledge for a debt. Remember, you were a bondman in Egypt, a hated race of aliens, yet I, Yehuway your God, redeemed you from thence."

"Thus, I command you to do this thing: whenever you cut down your harvest in your field, and have forgotten a sheaf in the field, do not go back to fetch it. Leave it for the stranger, for the fatherless, and for the widow so I, Yehuway your God, may bless you in all the work of your hands. When you beat the high braches of your olive tree, take only what has initially fallen for yourself. Do not go over again the boughs a second time. Let the fruit remain for the stranger, for the fatherless, and for the widow. When you gather the grapes of your vineyard, do not glean it after the initial gathering. Leave the remainder for the stranger, for the fatherless, and for the widow. Remember, that you were a bondman in the land of Egypt, an afflicted race of scorned aliens. Thus, I command you to do this thing."

ဆပ္သြဆပ္သြဆပ္ဆြဆပ္သြဆပ္သြ

"It must come to pass, if you desire to live in peace you must gather the first of all the fruits of the land from the allocations of farmland that I, Yehuway your God, gave you, and place it in a basket. Afterward, obey My decree, and journey to the land that I, Yehuway, have chosen. Place My name therein. Travel alongside the stranger in your journeys throughout the world and share whatever yo have with the stranger. It will be a spiritual blessing for you. Say to him, 'I profess this day to Yehuway my God, that I traversed to this country which Yehuway swore to our fathers and indeed he has given it to us.' Take the basket out of your hand and set it down before everyone in front of you and say before Me, Yehuway your God, 'My ancestor was a traveler: an Aramaean. He traveled through many lands to Egypt driven by famine. He sojourned to the saving land with his 11 sons (By this time Yoseph already held great power in Egypt with the title Zaphenath-paneah.) and 68 other loyal friends. There, in the province of Goshen, in the land of Egypt, my ancestors grew into a great nation: a powerful and mighty population. The

Egyptians' evil afflicted us. They laid upon us a hard bondage. When we petitioned Yehuway, the sole and exclusive God of our fathers, Yehuway heard our voice. He examined our affliction, our labor, our oppression. With compassion, Yehuway brought us out of Egypt, where we lived as an afflicted race of hated aliens. With a mighty hand, with an outstretched arm, and with great terror against the Egyptians He alone freed us! Yes, with miracles and with wonders He brought us into this place. He gave us this land: a land that flows with milk and honey. Now, behold, I have brought the first fruits of the land, which Yehuway has provided to me.'

"After you have spoken this thing, share your basket of fruit. Always worship Me, Yehuway your God. Then, with appreciation, rejoice in every good thing that I, Yehuway your God, have given to you. Do so in your house together with the stranger who has traveled into the land and lives among you. Let everyone know who Yehuway is and what I have performed for the Children of Abraham. Do so, so the stranger may find it in his heart to also worship and love Me as his own God.

"Listen to My voice. Perform everything according to everything that I have instructed you on.

"Recite this prayer every day of your lives:

'Yehuway, look down from Your holy habitation:
  from heaven,
      and bless your people Yisra'el, and the land
that You have given us,
  just as You had sworn to our fathers: a land that flows
with milk and honey.'

"This day, I, Yehuway your God, has commanded you to obey these statutes and judgments. Thus, you must keep and perform them with all your heart – and with all your soul.

"You have avouched Me, Yehuway, this day to be your God – to walk in My ways, to keep My statutes and My commandments as well as My judgments, and to listen to My voice.

"In turn, I, Yehuway have avouched you this day to be My treasured people, as I have promised. For this reason, you should keep all My commandments so I may place you high above all the nations of the world; on the very earth that I have created. Thus, in praise, and in name, and in honor, so you may remain a holy people to Me, Yehuway your God, as I have spoken, daily affirm to Me your sacred pledge."

ᔖᎧᏇᔖᎧᏇᔖᎧᏇᔖᎧᏇᔖᎧᏇ

After this, Mikha'el the Archangel retreated into the clouds which soon dissipated.

ᔖᎧᏇᔖᎧᏇᔖᎧᏇᔖᎧᏇᔖᎧᏇ

This is the song the Israelites sang after they settled into the western encampment that night:

"When Yisra'el journeyed out of Egypt, the House of Yaakov stemmed from a people speaking a strange language;
Judah was his sanctuary, Yisra'el his dominion.

The sea understood Judah's purpose. The Sea fled.
Yes, the river Jordan was driven back.
    The Mountains skipped like rams,
        the little hills like lambs.
What distressed you,
    O Sea,
        that you fled?
    Yes, river Jordan, what fear encumbered you that
you were driven back?
        Mountains skipped like rams and little hills
quaked like lambs!
    Tremble,
    O Earth,
        at the presence of Yehuway!
        at the presence of the God of
Yaakov
        Who turned the rock into a
sting of water
        And the flint into
small watery fountains."

ഽഠൢഽഠൢഽഠൢൢഠൢഽഠൢ

Samuel the prophet's poetic speech:

Israelite warriors!
Cease cutting off the hair from your temples, for it is
consecrated to God. Let it grow long to fortify your
courage and hide the fear of your eyes away from your
enemies.

Praise Yehuway for He avenges Yisra'el! People, join
our forces with willing desire and with an unhesitating
resolve. Hear, O you kings, give ear, O you princes, I, even
I, a woman gloried with the abilities of holy

manifestation, will sing to Yehuway! I will sing praises to Yehuway God of Yisra'el.

Yehuway, when you traveled out of the mountainous regions between the Dead Sea and the Gulf of 'Aqaba known to us as Seir, a land brimming with Horites and Edomites and Amalekites, yes, when you marched victoriously among all the unwanted and inglorious tribes residing in the fields of Edom,
　the earth trembled and the heavens dropped,
　　the clouds dropped water.
　　　the hill countries melted in front of the glorious strength of Yehuway,
　　　　even the Sinai that stood in front of Yehuway,
　God of Yisra'el, quaked.

In the days of Shamgar the son of Anath,
　in the days of Ya'el,
　　the oft-traveled caravans abandoned the main roads.
　Though vacant, desolate, unoccupied,
　　the travelers preferred to walk through remote byways.

Deborah speaks:
"The inhabitants of the villages ceased,
　they ceased in Yisra'el!

　"A cruel emptiness overpowered the land.

"Then I, Deborah, stood up,
　I became a mother for all the Children of Yisra'el.

"The betraying Children of Yisra'el chose new gods to worship,

    For this perpetrated deceit, war came upon the gates,

        yet what godly warrior could be found carrying a shield or a spear of righteousness among forty thousand in Yisra'el?

"My heart remains true to the Clan Leaders of Yisra'el

"For now,

    they are willing to offer themselves to lead the people into divine sanctification.

    "Praise Yehuway.

"I command:

Speak to those who ride on the less than perfect donkeys: the donkeys' hide that is an orange-brown color tinged with hair ends of gold.

Speak, those of you privileged to sit in judgment.

    Speak, those of you who walk by the waysides of the remote paths.

        Speak, those of you who are unburdened from the noise of archers in the places of drawing water.

"Together, rehearse and chant praises of the righteous acts of Yehuway.

"Even the righteous acts toward the inhabitants of His villages in Yisra'el.

    Only after this,

    will the warriors of Yehuway march in valor to the village gates."

Awake, awake, Deborah!
Awake!
Awake!
   Utter a song!

Rise, Barak!
   Lead your captives, son of Abinoam.

Yehuway created His firstborn, Mikha'el the Archangel,
   Who lives since the Day of Creation,
      to have dominion over the nobles among the people.

The First-Created speaks:

   "Yehuway made me to have dominion over the mighty!"

Samuel the prophet speaks:
"These are the five loyal tribes of Yehuway!

"Out of Ephraim came those raised by parents of seasoned warfare
   against Amalek.
Yes, their roots stem from the experience of their warring parents upon the Amalekites!
   Following Ephraim, rose the tribe of Benjamin to war beside the Ephraimites,
   Out of Machir approached the governors.
   Out of Zebulun,
      those who handle the pen of the writer."
The prince of Issachar joined Deborah,
   Yes, even Issachar as well as Barak,
      who was sent on foot into the valley.

There awaited the clans of Reuben.
These same ones approached Barak with great
thoughts of the heart.

"Why do you live among the sheepfolds?" Barak
asked.
"To hear the bleating of the flocks?"

In spite of Barak's pleas the clans of Reuben
continued to engage in a great searching of their hearts.

Gilead lived beyond the Jordan River,
so why did Dan remain in ships?

Asher continued thriving on the seashore while he
lived in the comfort of his beach houses.

Meanwhile,
in great contrast,
Zebulun and Naphtali jeopardized their
lives
even to the sacrifice of death in the
high places of the field.

The Clan leaders of the Five Righteous States traveled
forth
to fight the Kings of Canaan in Taanach,
near the waters of Megiddo;

They took no spoils of money.

Heavenly forces joined our battle.
They fought from heaven,

the stars held their divine course of
righteousness
in their battle against the demons pledged to
Sisera.

The river of Kishon swept Sisera's chariots and
infantry away,
that ancient river,
the river Kishon.

O my soul, march ever forward with grand strength.

Then the horses' hoofs broke,
through the means of the prancing of their mighty
ones.

"Curse Meroz!" said Mikha'el the Archangel, for they
failed to rally.

This said Yehuway's representative angel on earth:

"Curse bitterly the inhabitants who live in that
cowardly village
because they refused to help Yehuway,
to help Yehuway against the mighty."

Rather, praise the women of Yisra'el!

Blessed above women is Ya'el,
Wife of Heber the Kenite,
Blessed is she above all the women in every tent of
the land.

Sisera asked for water.
Ya'el gave him milk:

she brought out curds in a princely bowl.

As Sisera slept
    Ya'el placed her hand around a tent stake.
        With her right hand wrapped around a
worker's hammer,
            she struck Sisera.

She crushed his head,
    when she pierced and struck the long stake
through his temples.

At her feet he bowed,
    he fell where he laid;

        at her feet he bowed,
            he fell where he bowed;

    there, he fell down dead.

The mother of Sisera peered out the window and
cried through the lattice separating men from women,
"Why is his chariot so long in coming? Why so late the
clatter of the wheels of his chariot?"

Her wise women answered her,
    and she repeated to herself the wise woman's
sayings:
    "Have they not sped forward to war? Are they not
now dividing the prey, to every man a damsel or two,
    to Sisera a spoil of dyed colors,
        a spoil of embroidered colors of needlework,
            of embroidered colors of needlework on
both sides,

for the necks of those who take the spoil?"

In this manner, let all your enemies perish, O Yehuway!

But let those who love Him act as the sun rising in might!

www.ingramcontent.com/pod-product-compliance
Lightning Source LLC
Chambersburg PA
CBHW030447290526
45786CB00001B/479